Our Landscape May Forever Be
But Our Spirit Will Forever Be Strong!

MW00653847

SMB
Southwest Missouri Bank
HELPING REBUILD
JOPLIN!
We Can Do That!

Southwest Missouri Bank

800.943.8488 • smbonline.com

Joplin • Carthage • Duquesne • Neosho • Jasper • Alba

 Member FDIC

Like so many of you, the rebuilding process at St. John's Mercy continues at full speed and full strength. Our entire Mercy Joplin team is moving swiftly with more purpose than ever before. Our roster of Mercy doctors has actually grown despite this temporary setback, while our electronic health record system is performing exactly as we envisioned. We are currently working on our new 120-bed component hospital and we are working with the community on St. John's Mercy Hospital's permanent location. We are as committed to Joplin today as the Sisters were 126 years ago. **We stand as one with everyone in this community, and we will rise together.**

Thank You

In May, we saw the lives of our Joplin family turned upside down by the tornado. We would like to thank the police, fire fighters, emergency personnel, and volunteers in Joplin and across the region for the heroism they displayed in the aftermath of the tornado.

Building an infrastructure for the future of Joplin has been a part of our business for many years. We are happy to be a part of the rebuilding effort and to continue to serve our customers in Joplin for many years to come.

At Missouri American Water, our customers are family.

MISSOURI
AMERICAN WATER

WE CARE ABOUT WATER. IT'S WHAT WE DO.
(866) 430-0820 • www.missouriamwater.com

32 MINUTES IN MAY

The Joplin Tornado

32 Minutes in May

The Joplin Globe | www.joplinglobe.com

Mike Beatty | Publisher

Scott Meeker | Editor

Bill Caldwell | Photo Editor

Wally Kennedy, Emily Younker, Alexandra Rose Nicolas, Josh Letner, Roger McKinney, Joe Hadsall, Susan Redden, Debby Woodin, Jeff Lehr, Jim Henry, Mike Pound, Kelsey Ryan, Carol Stark and Kevin McClintock | Contributing writers

Kellen Jenkins | Staff photo

Pediment Publishing | Design and production

ACKNOWLEDGEMENTS

THE JOPLIN GLOBE STAFF WOULD like to thank the following people for their contributions to this project – Brad Belk, director of the Joplin Museum Complex; Ross Brown, creator of the Historic Joplin website; the National Weather Service and National Severe Storms Laboratory; the Associated Press; Caitlin Miller; and Charles Gibbons, whose "Angling in the Archives" collection remains a wonderful trip back into Joplin's yesteryear.

This book is dedicated to the 162 lives lost to the storm; to those who survived and whose lives were touched by the tragedy; and to those who came running to our city's aid in its wake.

A Message from the Publisher

WE AT THE JOPLIN GLOBE are proud to serve our community. The very night of the storm, our staff – many of whom lost everything – came to work to write the stories … your stories, our stories. They came in soaking wet, in flip-flops and T-shirts.

Having been in the newspaper business most of my life, there has never been anything of more importance to cover than the May 22 tornado and the rebuilding of Joplin. As we continue to rebuild, it will be our responsibility and duty to keep you abreast of the latest news and information that will affect our recovery.

I know that Joplin is resilient and that the tornado will not defeat us. I am so proud of everyone who works for The Joplin Globe. We have taken great pride in being there for you every step of the way.

Mike Beatty

Publisher

At Ninth and Joplin.
Telephone pole on street car at Tenth and Main.
Plate glass broken at Roosevelt Flats.
At Eleventh and Main.
Baptist Church.

ABOVE: An illustration from an issue of the Joplin News Herald shows an artist's rendering of the damage Joplin sustained during the April 19, 1902, tornado. *Courtesy Historic Joplin*

LEFT: A frame taken from video shows the tornado on the ground May 22 just west of Joplin. It ultimately plowed all the way across Joplin, and into Duquesne and beyond. *Courtesy The Associated Press*

PHOTOGRAPHERS

Curtis Almeter

"Among the many horrors I saw (the night of May 22), I remember a woman walking around the foundation of a home calling out for her missing son. Her voice was hoarse and her initial panic had since been replaced with despair as she repeated his name. I prayed he was still alive but suspected the worst as I continued walking down the street. Later, I would read his name in a list of confirmed dead.

The photographs I took the following days were not just images of strangers. They were mothers and fathers, coworkers or neighbors. They were regular people like you or I, trying to cope after having their lives turned upside down. It was their faces that represented a desperate city in time of need."

As a freelance photojournalist, Curtis Almeter has taken photos for The Cass County Conservative, The Joplin Globe, The Neosho Daily News, The Chart and the Crowder College Sentry.

T. Rob Brown

"Covering the aftermath of the tornado was an experience like no other. Not just because I was covering one of the most devastating events of my life, but because I was also affected. The May 22 tornado displaced me and my brother from our home and destroyed my car. Through that experience, I was able to better relate to others affected by this tragedy."

T. Rob Brown has been with The Joplin Globe since 2000. Before that, he was the photo editor of the Branson Daily News from 1997 to 2000. He has covered multiple presidential visits, plane crashes, the Big Red One at Fort Riley, Kan., Whiteman Air Force Base (home of the B-2 Stealth Bomber), a police shootout and much more during his 18-year career in daily newspapers

Mike Gullett

"None of the assignments or news events I've covered prepared me for what I saw and photographed the evening of May 22, and the days that followed. The destruction was as far as the eye could see and the people that evening were in shock, as was I. I looked for people to photograph. Most were walking or helping others walk. I spent the next four days photographing the destruction, cleanup and volunteers. It was like making photos was my way of dealing with the devastation experienced by my neighbors and town. I shoot some events and the continued cleanup in Joplin a couple of times a week. I plan to document the rebuilding of Joplin throughout the weeks, months and years to come."

Mike Gullett has been a photojournalist for 35 years. After 25 years working as a photographer at four newspapers in Southeast Kansas and Southwest Missouri, he began teaching photojournalism full time and continues to freelance for news agencies and organizations.

Roger Nomer

"I've been on the scene right after a tornado strike before, most recently in 2008 in Newton County. But I've never witnessed utter destruction like I saw on May 22, stretching as far as I could see in all directions. It was frightening, overwhelming and most of all it didn't seem real. What struck me the most as I got out of my car was the dead silence. There were car alarms sounding and water gushing from broken pipes, but overall it was eerily quiet. Honestly, from that point on, the night becomes a total blur in my memory. Only by looking through the photos that I shot that night can I remember any details at all."

Roger Nomer has been a staff photographer with the Joplin Globe for over six years. Perviously, he worked for newspapers in Johnson County, Eudora, Kan., and Lawrence, Kan. He graduated from the University of Kansas with a bachelor's degree in journalism in 2000. He has documented many other tornados in the area, including the Newton County tornado in 2008, for which he won several awards for his photo coverage.

Bill Shepherd

"On May 22, 2011, I was nine blocks away from the EF-5 tornado at home with my wife and daughter, peering out our basement and listening to the most terrifying sounds we have ever heard. I quickly grabbed my camera … I became a first responder who was also a photojournalist trying to make sense of the sheer scale of the event. To date I have taken more than 15,000 images of the storm's aftermath and still deal with the guilt about things I should or shouldn't have done the night of the tornado. I saw neighbors saving neighbors and heroes in every direction. I will never forget how my fellow citizens rallied in their greatest time of need and answered the call of humanity."

A Joplin native, Bill Shepherd has been a freelance photojournalist for the Joplin Globe for four years. He served in the U.S. Army infantry during Desert Storm, and graduated from Missouri Southern State University in 2005 with a degree in communications, with an emphasis on journalism.

Curtis Almeter

T. Rob Brown

Mike Gullett

Roger Nomer

Bill Shepherd

TABLE OF CONTENTS

FOREWORD 7

1 - SIX MILES OF TERROR 9

2 - THE SCIENCE OF THE TORNADO 39

3 - BACK IN BUSINESS 43

4 - OPERATION RISING EAGLE 49

5 - THE MEDICAL COMMUNITY 57

6 - JOPLIN'S PET PROJECT 63

7 - ROOTING FOR THE HOME TEAM 69

8 - HELPING HANDS 75

9 - DEATH DOES NOT GET THE LAST WORD 91

10 - FACES OF THE STORM 98

11 - WINDS OF CHANGE 121

FOREWORD

There were no sirens, no advance warnings for the residents of Joplin as the storm rolled through the area.

As Mother Nature's fury was unleashed in the form of a powerful tornado, trees were torn from the earth, buildings were destroyed, telephone poles were snapped like twigs and homes were reduced to little more than splinters.

"Carrying death and destruction in its wake, a cyclone passed over Joplin yesterday," the Joplin Globe would report the following day. "Accompanied by rain and hail the fierce wind swept over the city for upwards of an hour, bringing terror to those who suffered nothing more severe. Semi-darkness, intermittent flashes of lighting and the sullen boom of distant thunder added to the horror of the situation, contributing pyrotechnic features rivaling the most sensational stage storms seen in the wildest of melodramas.

"Telephonic and telegraphic communication with the outside world was all but annihilated, the street car service was paralyzed and the city left in darkness so far as the electric service was concerned … Before the flying mass of sleet and water, bill boards, shattered glass and torn roofs that swept through the streets like a deadly cannonade men, women and children had fallen."

The tornado claimed the life of 2-year-old Esther Hunter, and critically injured several other residents.

That was Saturday, April 19, 1902.

It wasn't the first to strike Joplin – at least two people had been killed by a tornado that touched down in May 1883 – nor would it be the last for the Southwest Missouri town, which sits just outside the region that has come to be known as "Tornado Alley."

One person was killed and at least 60 injured when a tornado ripped through the heart of Joplin on Wednesday, May 5, 1971. Several blocks wide, it moved northeast through town, just missing Missouri Southern State College.

Between 1,500 and 1,600 buildings, homes and businesses were damaged. Then Gov. Warren Hearnes declared the city a disaster area, with damages estimated to exceed $20 million.

Two years later, three people died when a tornado touched down in the early morning hours of Friday, May 11, 1973. Creating winds that reached between 70 and 100 mph, it caused extensive damage throughout the city. Jasper and Newton counties were declared disaster areas by Gov. Kit Bond, with damages in Joplin estimated at $12.8 million.

The next tornado to strike within city limits came on Sunday, April 28, 1996 – an EF-1 that peeled away roofs, tossed cars, trucks and trailers when it passed over South Range Line, between 32nd Street and Interstate 44.

Nearby towns have also been hard hit in recent years. The devastating tornadoes of Sunday, May 4, 2003, ripped through Carl Junction, Stockton and Pierce City. That storm system killed 24 people and injured nearly 200 in Missouri and Kansas. Twenty-three area people lost their lives on Saturday, May 10, 2008, when a deadly tornado crossed through Northeast Oklahoma and into Southwest Missouri.

They are dates forever etched into the minds of those who lived through them. Those who lost loved ones. Those who lost homes. Those who saw everything they owned scattered to the winds.

But there's a spirit of resiliency in times of trial that comes naturally to Joplin-area residents, says Brad Belk, director of the Joplin Museum Complex.

It's a quality that developed from the town's hardscrabble mining heritage – a survival instinct born from those who worked to bring the riches of lead and zinc up from the earth and turn what was a group of mining camps into a thriving community.

"They always rallied, regardless of what obstacle (they faced)," said Belk. "Any time there was a cave-in, the mines virtually stopped in the Tri-State Mining District and miners rallied to the site to do whatever they could to free however many men were trapped.

"Mining was a tough job. It took discipline, dedication and resourcefulness. It also came with rejection and failure. You had to have the mindset for it. And that community spirit is still here and more evident than ever. People have rolled up their sleeves and pitched in to help in any way they can. We've always rallied. We've always come back from whatever catastrophe (has struck)."

As the storm clouds gathered in the west on the afternoon of Sunday, May 22, 2011, that spirit would once again be put to the test by a tornado that carved through the city without mercy.

In just 32 minutes, it created two distinct chapters in Joplin's history: Life before that date, and life after.

OPPOSITE: Residents at a mobile home park try to salvage belongings after the tornado that struck Joplin on May 11, 1973. *Photo by Globe file*

Chapter One

SIX MILES OF TERROR

THE TORNADO CRAWLED ACROSS JOPLIN.

Most tornados blow through towns, some at speeds of 50 miles per hour.

Not the EF-5 that hit Joplin on May 22, 2011.

It rolled slowly, minute after agonizing minute, mile after agonizing mile.

An EF-5 is the most powerful of storms. On that day, the tornado stayed on the ground in Joplin for six miles, churning up neighborhoods, businesses, churches, schools, homes and lives. Three-quarters of a mile wide at times, the slow-moving tornado ground up everything before it.

The toll: an estimated 8,000 structures, roughly 400 businesses and 4,500 jobs affected, more than 1,150 injured and 162 lives lost.

Joplin was eviscerated.

Maybe Bill Davis, the head meteorologist with the National Weather Service station in Springfield, said it best: He called the tornado "a fist coming out of the sky."

SOUTH SCHIFFERDECKER

According to radar and initial field reports, the tornado touched down at 5:41 p.m., near West 32nd Street and Central City Road.

Within minutes, it claimed one of its first victims.

Eighteen-year-old Will Norton and his father, Mark, were driving to their home in the Arbor Hills subdivision following Will's high school graduation ceremony at the Leggett & Platt Athletic Center. As they approached their home on Old Orchard Road, the fist bore down. Mark asked his son to pull over.

Father and son were both wearing seat belts. They clutched each other as their Hummer H3 was tossed and battered by wind and debris. In the roaring chaos, Will was pulled from his father's arms. It was the last time he was seen alive.

In the coming days, authorities and family members scoured the area, searched for Will in area hospitals and set up a Facebook account: "Help Find Will Norton." The site received thousands of posts.

Mark was taken to Freeman West with injuries that included a broken arm, injuries family members believe were caused by his desperate efforts to hold on to his son.

Days later, family friend and former Joplin firefighter Steve Lea watched as rescuers searched two debris-choked ponds along Schifferdecker for victims.

"They were so close (to home)." Lea said. "Five seconds would have made so much difference, maybe even three seconds."

The family announced Saturday, May 28, that Will's body had been found in one of the ponds.

2423 W. 26TH ST.

Becky Burris was slicing strawberries in the kitchen at St. Paul's United Methodist Church that evening. Like a lot of people on the east sides of buildings that day, she was unaware of the storm's approach.

Although the tornado ripped off much of the roof and tore away an entire wall of the church, Burris didn't get so much as a scratch.

2600 BLOCK OF SOUTH MONROE

Larry Eller and his wife, Chris, lost their home that Sunday. Sifting through the rubble two days later, Larry located a box of valuables that had been spared, but he was searching for something else.

"I'd like to find my passport," Larry said. "I want to go to Europe next week."

They rode out the storm in their basement, hiding under the stairs. The events were too much for Chris to talk about as she gingerly stepped through the debris that was once her living room.

"We got down to the door and then everything hit," Larry said. "We knew we were in trouble when we looked up through the floor and saw lightning."

The Ellers have no plans to move.

"We'll rebuild," he said. "It's a good neighborhood with good people. We'll rebuild and come back stronger."

1802 W. 26TH ST.

The Joplin Elks Lodge was scheduled to hold its weekly bingo game on Sunday. Had the tornado struck a few hours later, 50 people might have been inside.

Rescuers removed five Elks who had taken refuge in the lodge. Only one survived, said Kevin Keys, head trustee of the lodge.

Like St. Paul's, the Elks is a charitable organization that the community leans on in time of need, but the devastation has left the group reeling. As Keys later surveyed the landscape around the lodge, he was unsure what the immediate future would hold, but then added: "We'll be back. We'll regroup. We've got over 500 members so we'll be back."

2602 MCCLELLAND BLVD.

Rance Junge was working at the Pronto Pharmacy on Sunday night. He was unable to see the

---

OPPOSITE: A view looking west down 26th Street after the tornado hit Joplin. *Photo by Mike Gullett*

storm approaching because the pharmacy did not have windows facing west.

"We didn't have any hail and it didn't look threatening on this side," Junge said. "When I opened up the back door, I saw a wall and heard a huge noise, so I knew it was coming."

Junge's first instinct was to take shelter at St. John's Regional Medical Center, but the tornado was on top of him.

When Junge and a co-worker ran to the front of the store to make their escape he was confronted with a chilling image. A motorist who saw the storm approaching was attempting to turn around in front of the store, but was gripped with fear.

"I could tell they were terrified by what they were seeing," Junge said. "He tried to turn around in a panic but didn't make it. He didn't have time to get in and we didn't have time, the door pulled out of my hand and I knew we weren't going to make it across the street."

They took refuge in the store's bathroom. The pair held onto plumbing to keep from being swept away.

"The building lifted, exploded, it did everything," Junge said. "And then we were in the eye of the thing for a while because it calmed down and I thought, 'Oh gosh, we made it.' We could see daylight and there wasn't a lot of building left, but then we got hit by the back side of it and that was when I got hit with debris in the back. I couldn't protect my back and my head, and I got clubbed by stuff."

He tilted his head slightly forward to display dark purple bruises that protruded from the collar of his shirt.

TOP RIGHT: Rescuers look for survivors in the rubble of the Payless shoe store on Range Line following the tornado. *Photo by Roger Nomer*

RIGHT: Tornado survivors walk down Range Line Road on the evening of May 22. *Photo by Roger Nomer*

ABOVE: Academy Sports on Range Line Road was among the businesses devastated by the tornado. *Photo by Roger Nomer*

The terrified motorist was nowhere to be seen.

"I don't think he made it, I think he went up in it," Junge said.

ST. JOHN'S REGIONAL MEDICAL CENTER

To get a sense of the EF-5's power, consider: St. John's Regional Medical Center, one of the biggest buildings in Joplin, shifted four inches off of its foundation, according to Missouri Gov. Jay Nixon. The damage was so severe that the hospital was unusable at the precise moment it was needed most.

According to reports, some emergency room patients were sucked out into the parking lot. Hospital staff began evacuating 183 patients along with much of the equipment and supplies that were later used at the emergency triage center set up at Memorial Hall.

At least nine people died in the the hospital.

2502 S. MOFFET AVE.

Sandy Conlee came out of her house immediately after the storm hit and saw a resident from the Greenbriar Nursing Home wandering down 26th Street.

"One of the little old men from the nursing home was standing in the middle of the street when we came out of the house," Conlee said. "He had blood all over his head. He was in shock."

Conlee said her brother and two sons joined in the search for survivors. They were shocked by the carnage that greeted them.

"There were bodies and broken bones and blood and stuff."

Ten bodies were removed from the rubble of the nursing home. An excavator was needed to remove a minivan that had crashed through the roof of one room.

2415 S. MOFFET AVE.

St. Mary's Catholic Church, the rectory, the parish center, the adjacent Catholic elementary school, even the nearby frame house that served as the original

church more than 70 years ago — all were destroyed. Steel was twisted into a mass of metal and insulation that looked like a Brillo pad.

Bishop James Johnston, of the Catholic Diocese of Springfield-Cape Girardeau, said the school lost members of one family — a father and his two daughters who took refuge in the Home Depot on Range Line Road. They were members of St. Peter the Apostle Catholic Church, he said.

But the large iron cross — which has withstood previous tornadoes — was still towering above the fields of debris, soon to become a much-photographed icon in the aftermath.

300 BLOCK OF EAST 22ND STREET

Not long after the storm, Kent Gilbreth stood in the street in front of the shattered remnants of his father's home, his blue eyes fixed in what combat veterans describe as the "thousand-yard stare." This is the neighborhood that his father had lived in for 40 years.

Gilbreth took shelter in the corner of his father's

basement as the tornado plowed through the neighborhood.

"It sounded like a huge train," he said. "I saw a black wall and got down to the basement just before it hit. I felt the suction and thought (I was) getting sucked out for a second. I got glass stuck everywhere."

As the father and son loaded what few possessions they could salvage into the bed of a truck, Gilbreth was unsure of their next move.

"We'll just take it one day at a time," he said.

2104 INDIANA AVE.

Looking east from the Gilbreth home, much of the tornado's path spread open in a vista of complete destruction. The remains of Joplin High School and the nearby Franklin Tech Center were evident. It

---

ABOVE: A broken water main amid the tornado debris sends a fountain into the air. *Photo by Roger Nomer*

would be easy to believe that the buildings had been the target of an airstrike.

The complete destruction of four schools and damage to several other buildings would bring Superintendent C.J. Huff to the edge of tears in a press conference two days later.

2300 BLOCK OF SOUTH WISCONSIN

Jennifer and Danny Moore and their two children said they felt lucky to be alive as they retrieved belongings from their flattened home.

Danny Moore and his daughter were returning from a trip to Home Depot when the city's tornado sirens sounded for the second time.

"It was just pitch black and there was debris flying, but I didn't know what it was because this is the first tornado I've lived through," Danny said.

But his wife, Jennifer, knew the danger that was closing in.

"My husband and daughter were just pulling up in the drive and I looked over and saw it and had enough time to grab (the kids) and throw them in the bathtub and we laid down on top of them," she said. "And then it started sucking us up and we just gripped the tub and held on and we thought we were through it because it calmed and you looked up and saw clear and the next thing you know, you saw it coming again.

"(Danny) was getting ready to get up and I said, 'No, we've got to lay back down because that's the eye of it.'"

Buried under debris, the family was freed by a neighbor. They then joined the effort to free others.

TOP LEFT: The view from 17th Street and Range Line not long after the tornado hit the area. *Photo by Roger Nomer*

LEFT: The path of the tornado is shown along Range Line. *Photo by Roger Nomer*

2021 HAMPSHIRE TERRACE

Like many others, Rebecca Wilkinson and her daughter rode out the tornado in the bathroom.

"I got a call from my mother and she said to take cover, so I grabbed a blanket and headed to the bathroom," she said. "By the time I shut the door, it hit."

Wilkinson huddled with her young daughter as her apartment collapsed. The two were saved from the crushing weight of debris by her toilet and sink. As she and her daughter laid under the rubble following the tornado, she could hear her terrified neighbors cry for help.

"All I could hear were screams," she said.

Eventually, rescuers got to them.

"I handed my daughter out through a hole, and then an elderly gentleman came and pulled me out."

3110 E. 20TH ST.

Home Depot was no match for the full fury of the EF-5, its winds spinning in excess of 200 miles per hour.

Seven people were killed when the store was hit.

Throughout much of the week, urban search and

BELOW: Emergency vehicles line up along northbound Range Line as rescue efforts get under way. *Photo by Roger Nomer*

ABOVE: Joplin Police Sgt. Gabe Allen carries 11-year-old Aspen Bowman to safety from the remains of Academy Sports. *Photo by Roger Nomer*

rescue crews looked for survivors with concrete saws, jackhammers, rescue dogs and fiber-optic cameras that snaked into dark spaces and under large concrete slabs that comprised the store's front wall.

Rescue efforts were hampered by heavy rain showers early in the week. According to rescuers, rain washes away the scent left by survivors and makes it difficult for dogs. Despite the adverse conditions, the crews pressed on.

After getting the call Sunday evening, the rescue team was on the road within an hour. They arrived in

RIGHT: Emergency workers load a patient into a waiting ambulance following the tornado.

Photo by Roger Nomer

BELOW: Corrugated metal siding was wrapped around a pole by the force of the storm. *Photo by Roger Nomer*

Joplin after midnight and went to work at 3 a.m. After searching for nearly 15 hours, the exhausted team was forced to rest. According to team leader Doug Westhoff, the Joplin tornado was one of the worst disasters the unit has seen.

"This is a devastating event," he said. "We've been to the World Trade Center, Hurricane Katrina twice, and Hurricane Ike. This is a significant weather event. This is Mother Nature telling us who's in charge."

DUQUESNE

Duquesne was next in line.

The tornado destroyed more than 250 homes, 50 of Duquesne's 100 businesses, and killed several residents.

Police Chief Tommy Kitch said that 60 to 70 percent of the town was gone.

3425 JAGUAR ROAD

By the time the storm reached the rural home of

Randy and Cindy Wagner, the couple had had ample warning and time to get their family into a crawl space.

Wagner pulled a 150-pound concrete cover closed as the tornado approached. As the storm passed

---

ABOVE: A Bible is set out in the sun to dry after being salvaged from St. Paul's United Methodist Church. *Photo by Roger Nomer*

over, it pulled the heavy door off and flung it into the yard causing the family to crawl farther under the house. Randy said he could feel the tornado sucking him out the opening. He braced himself against the foundation and held on to his home's floor joists. After the storm had passed he crawled out and viewed the damage. Although he lost more than 20 majestic oak trees, and suffered extensive roof, fence, window and landscaping damage, Wagner considers himself lucky. His immediate and extended family were safe, his home was insured and he quickly received help from family and friends.

"We're very fortunate and we are praying for the people in Joplin because we know they lost everything," he said.

KODIAK ROAD

Thirty-two minutes after first touching down, the tornado finally lifted near Diamond – having been on the ground for nearly 13 miles.

In those 32 minutes, the tornado forever changed the face of Joplin and the surrounding region.

Nearly 7,000 homes destroyed.

More than 400 businesses and 4,500 jobs affected.

More than 1,150 injured, 162 lives lost.

The fist had done its work. ■

***

RIGHT: Bob Harbottle, who lost his Joplin home, gets a hug from fellow church member Wendy Chapman during a community prayer service held May 25 at the Joplin Family Worship Center. *Photo by T. Rob Brown*

ABOVE: Four-year-old Griffan Keller clutches onto a teddy bear and his father, Travis Keller, during a Q&A session held outside the American Red Cross shelter at Missouri Southern State University. The Kellers lost their home on South Virginia Avenue. *Photo by T. Rob Brown*

RIGHT: Jesse Bruce shows where he and his family hid in their basement during the tornado. The floor of their home turned into a protective shield over them as the storm passed.

Photo by T. Rob Brown

BOTTOM RIGHT: After losing his home and most of his possessions, Ronnie Irby said that he wasn't sure where his next stop would be once the Red Cross shelter he was staying at closed.

Photo by Roger Nomer

OPPOSITE: Rosie Sanders embraces Tyrone Townsend inside a new FEMA home east of Duquesne Road. The couple, who moved from shelter to shelter after their home on Michigan Avenue was destroyed by the tornado, said they were happy to finally have a place to call home.

Photo by T. Rob Brown

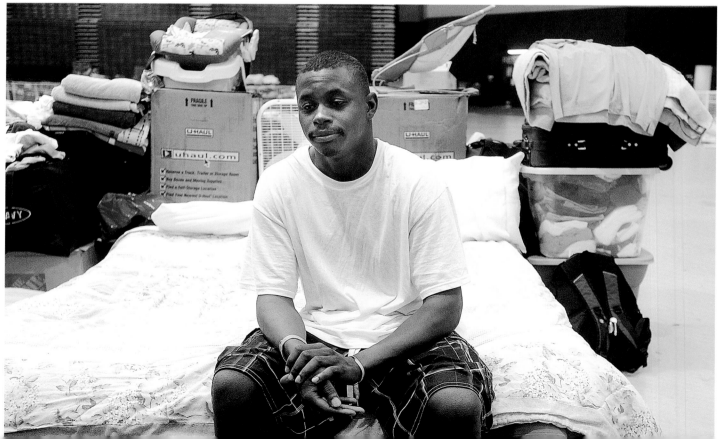

ABOVE: Residents survey the damage following the May 22 tornado. *Photo by B.W. Shepherd*

LEFT: Rescuers try to free a woman from a destroyed building. *Photo by Roger Nomer*

FAR LEFT: Rescuers look through a damaged building in search of survivors. *Photo by Roger Nomer*

LEFT: A woman gets assistance leaving the rubble of her Joplin home following the tornado. Many ordinary citizens offered help to those in need after the storm.

Photo by B.W. Shepherd

ABOVE: Covered with a blanket, a man trapped in the remains of a house near Parr Hill Park waits to be rescued. *Photo by B.W. Shepherd*

ABOVE: Bridgette Lough watches as search and rescue teams search for survivors in the remains of the Sonic Drive-In she managed. *Photo by Curtis Almeter*

ABOVE: A man looks for help for his wife, who was trapped in their family truck near 18th Street. *Photo by B. W. Shepherd*

ABOVE: A woman clutches her grandson near 20th Street and Rhode Island Avenue about an hour after the May 22 tornado. *Photo by B.W. Shepherd*

OPPOSITE: Desiree Rodgers is comforted by her fiance, Matthew Morris, after being rescued from under debris at Dillons grocery store. *Photo by B.W. Shepherd*

LEFT: A man carries his daughter through the disaster area wile searching for family members after the tornado. *Photo by B.W. Shepherd*

BELOW: A woman breaks down in tears while looking through a home destroyed near 20th Street and Connecticut Avenue. *Photo by B.W. Shepherd*

ABOVE: Shortly after the storm moved out of Joplin, residents began the difficult task of picking up the pieces, searching what was left of their homes to see what could be salvaged. *Photo by B.W. Shepherd*

RIGHT: Jeff Pyles pauses from his work of salvaging some of his belongings from his home two days after the tornado. He said that looting had been a problem in his neighborhood. *Photo by Mike Gullett*

FAR RIGHT: Robert and Mimi Pfeiffer – along with their children, Zacharia, 1, Kathryn, 3, and Christian, 4 – were among the Joplin families who found shelter at the Ignite.tv church. *Photo by Curtis Almeter*

ABOVE: "Courage" the stuffed bear was one of the many items salvaged in one tornado-stricken home on Highview Street. *Photo by Curtis Almeter*

OPPOSITE: A tricycle sits outside of a home that was ransacked by the EF-5 tornado. *Photo by Curtis Almeter*

LEFT: One of many reminders erected to encourage people to keep Joplin in their prayers. *Photo by Curtis Almeter*

OPPOSITE: Contractors with the U.S. Army Corps of Engineers clear a lot in the 2500 block of Pennsylvania Avenue.

Photo by Roger Nomer

37

Chapter Two

THE SCIENCE OF THE TORNADO

METEOROLOGISTS AREN'T EXACTLY SCRATCHING THEIR heads in disbelief, but they sure would like to know what caused a normal spring storm to produce a devastating tornado on the west side of Joplin in a matter of seconds.

They know that a series of storm mergers occurred about a half hour to 15 minutes before the tornado developed and that those mergers intensified the supercell thunderstorm that would produce the deadliest tornado since modern record keeping began in 1950.

They also know that observant radar operators in Springfield, without much evidence of a classic tornado hook on radar, detected rotation inside the storm and noticed that the main storm appeared to be making a gradual right turn. These important observations would prove to be crucial for the 24-minute advance warning that Joplin would receive.

But that's about all they know. They cannot see into the storm to see exactly what happened. But something happened.

"To get a tornado going is, in itself, a rare thing," said Bill Davis, head meteorologist with the National Weather Service station in Springfield.

"Now, just think about what it took to get that to happen with such a massive tornado.

"The mergers, if you will, added the steroids to this storm. We could have had an EF-2 or an EF-3 tornado without the merger. But something happened and it had to fit perfectly to produce this EF-5. The odds of that happening are astronomical.

"This is a tornado that was pieced together from several circulation mergers to make the perfect storm."

For two days before May 22, computer modeling by the Storm Prediction Center in Norman, Okla.,

suggested there was a 30-percent chance or slight risk of severe thunderstorms that day. It was not until May 22 that the National Weather Service upgraded the forecast to a moderate risk of severe weather.

The tornado risk did not become elevated until later in the day when extreme amounts of low-level convection became apparent.

There were some early signs. The upper-level jet stream was farther south than where it should be for late May. At the surface, a frontal boundary was sagging into Missouri. The dry line in Oklahoma had shifted to the east. The stage was set for severe weather, but nothing about that day would suggest what would unfold that afternoon.

"The forecast leading to the April 27 tornado outbreak across the Deep South and the forecast for Joplin on May 22 were fundamentally different," said Greg Carbin, lead meteorologoist at the Storm Prediction Center. "We knew a tornado outbreak would happen on April 27 with large, long-tracked and violent tornadoes. The forecast for Joplin was much more ambiguous. It was not considered an outbreak day.

"It was a typical day in May for widespread severe weather. This day in May in Joplin is what you would expect. Nothing really stood out."

Bill Gallus, a professor of meteorology at Iowa State University who is studying the Joplin tornado, said, "I was at a recent gathering of meteorologists in Boulder (Colo.). Many of them said that the one bad thing about the Joplin tornado was that it was not like any other EF-5.

"What you had was a bunch of storms come together. It did not look like a classic storm that would produce an EF-5. With most EF-5s, you see them coming. This tornado was wrapped in rain.

They did not recognize that it was a tornado until the roar was on them. Joplin did not see it coming."

When the main supercell thunderstorm emerged on May 22 in Labette County, Kan., it headed east, but showed a tendency to turn right. As it got closer to Joplin, the radar images show a system that is falling apart. Then, other cells form south or to the flank of the supercell. What happens next is what turned a summer storm into a killer.

Said Gallus: "Somehow those storms combined. We don't know what went on in there. But it organized so quickly."

Carbin said merging storms are not uncommon. When it does happen, it is more likely the storms will dissipate instead of becoming more powerful. But it does happen from time to time. The tornado that struck Pierce City in 2003 was formed when two storms came together. The tornado that struck Picher, Okla., in 2008 became more powerful when it joined another storm before entering Newton County.

"I would say that more than half the time these mergers cause destructive interference because it increases the disorganization of the storm," said Carbin.

Eric Wise, a meteorologist at the weather station in Springfield, issued his first tornado warning that day for an area north of Joplin at 5:09 p.m. when a

OPPOSITE: This image provided by the National Severe Storms Laboratory shows the storm rolling into Joplin on May 22. The smaller storms to its south quickly merged with the main supercell, resulting in the EF-5 tornado. *Image courtesy National Severe Storms Laboratory*

newly-formed cell joined with the supercell from Labette County. The city sounded its sirens at 5:11 p.m.

As Wise watches the radar, another cell merges with the supercell. It is this merger that will precipitate a massive tornado. He detects upward rotation in the storm on radar and has heard about funnel sightings in Cherokee County, Kan. With no clear evidence of a classic tornado hook visible on radar, he issues a blanket warning at 5:17 p.m. for all of Joplin because it appears the supercell is veering right. The city sounds its sirens again at 5:31 p.m.

The tornado hits Joplin at approximately 5:41 p.m. ■

TOP RIGHT: A view from 17th Street and Range Line after the tornado. *Photo by Roger Nomer*

RIGHT: An hour after the EF-5 tornado hit Joplin, people began filling the street a few block south of 20th Street as rescue workers arrived to search for survivors. *Photo by B.W. Shepherd*

ABOVE: An aerial view shows the path of devastation in the wake of the EF-5 tornado as it crossed Main Street. *Photo by Roger Nomer*

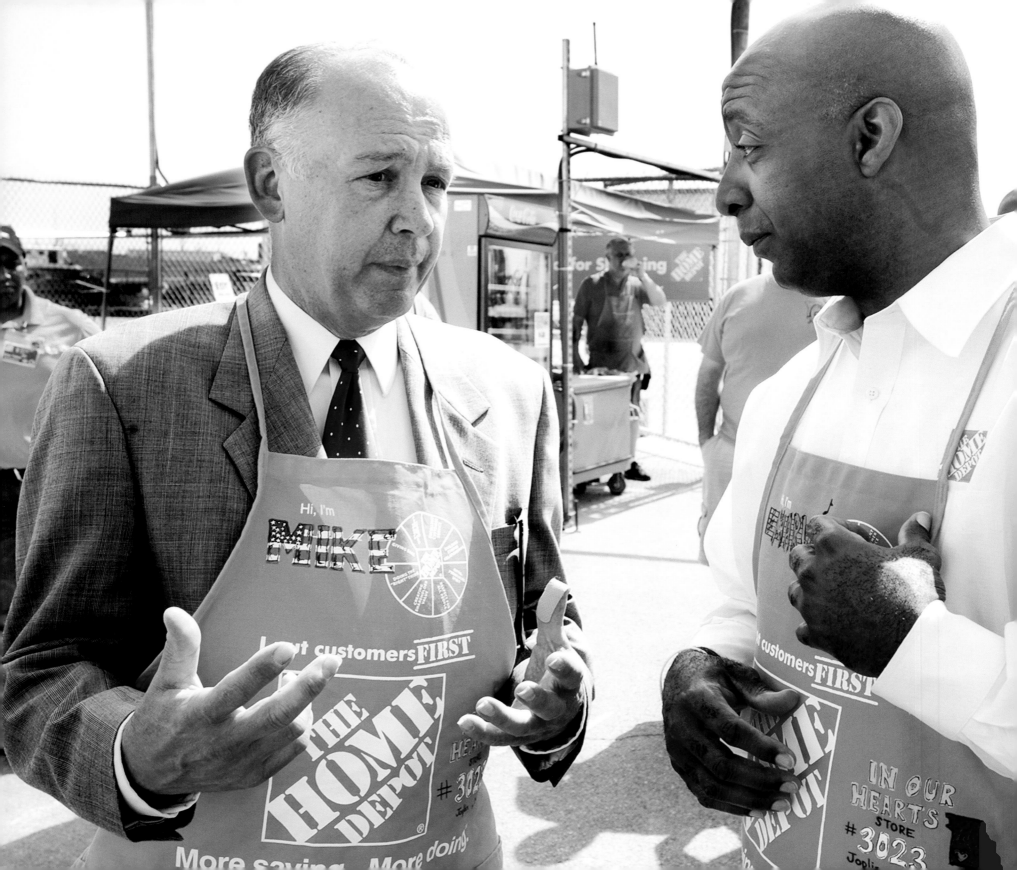

Chapter Three

BACK IN BUSINESS

A WEEK AFTER THE TORNADO, workers had applied a fresh coat of canary yellow paint to the exterior of Norma's Kitchen on South Main Street.

Owner Burim Hamiti estimated that the May 22 tornado did between $70,000 and $80,000 in damage to the restaurant.

Hamiti also lost his home and vehicles in the tornado, but he said that he was determined to rebuild. He has seen tough times before. His family 12 years ago emigrated from war-torn Kosovo to the U.S., and settled in Texas.

He was just one of hundreds of small-business owners who continued picking up the pieces in order to reopen. Rob O'Brian, president of the Joplin Area Chamber of Commerce, estimated that the tornado destroyed or severely damaged more than 400 Joplin businesses and affected up to 4,500 workers.

Still, he said, news of Joplin's demise was greatly exaggerated.

"I think the good news is that a number of businesses have already indicated that they intend to be back, if they're not already back," O'Brian said. "Our team here at the chamber, in the three weeks following the tornado, made personal contact, either face-to-face or by phone, with more than 400 of the businesses (located inside) the impacted area. The vast majority of them said they intend to be back."

Here, O'Brian paused to list a half-dozen employers, including Walgreens, Home Depot, Wal-Mart and St. John's Regional Medical Center.

"All have indicated they'll be back," he said.

By early July, less than two months after the tornado damaged or destroyed 450 businesses, approximately 150 had reopened, opened while still undergoing repairs or opened at new or temporary locations.

"For us to be (two months out) from the tornado, and already having so many of our businesses coming back, and so many others having announced their intentions to come back, it's a very positive thing for" Joplin and the entire region's business community, O'Brian said.

A number of resources quickly became available to help Joplin business owners with intermediate and longterm needs.

The Small Business Administration offered a program to assist business owners with damaged personal and real property (equipment, buildings) as well as so-called "economic injury" — loss of income caused by the loss of a business due to the storm. There was also help being provided by the Small Business and Technology Development Center, located at Missouri Southern State University.

Also, former U.S. Sen. John C. Danforth announced an effort to raise as much as $10 million from individuals, companies and foundations for a new non-profit organization called Joplin Tomorrow. The organization provides low or no-interest loans to businesses that want to locate in the vast area destroyed by the tornado.

Pages quickly formed on the social media site Facebook, allowing fans of local businesses to stay informed about rebuilding plans, or just to share their hopes that a favorite spot would rebuild. By mid-July, more than 3,100 people had "liked" the Rebuild Pizza By Stout page, and fans of Dude's Daylight Donuts watched for news of the start of rebuilding efforts there. The owners of Pizza by Stout would later announce that they would not rebuild.

Some business owners tried to look upon the need to rebuild as a positive.

Standing in what remained of the dining area of Jim Bob's Steak and Ribs, Stacy Gamble assessed the damage from the storm. Her first thought was for her customers; she considers them to be her extended family.

"Our customers are like our family," she said. "It's devastating, but to have been closed (when the tornado struck) is a blessing."

Gamble came of age working in her father's restaurant. She sees the destruction as a chance to make some changes to the Joplin landmark.

"Our goal as we rebuild the whole thing is to go back to the old Jim Bob's," she said. "You know, with the old wood floors. We're looking at it as an opportunity. That's the only thing you can do." ∎

OPPOSITE: Mayor Mike Woolston (left) speaks with Home Depot's Executive Vice President of Sales Marvin Ellison. The Range Line business quickly created a temporary store to serve customers.

Photo by T. Rob Brown

ABOVE: Dillons grocery store, shortly after it was struck by the May 22 tornado. *Photo by B.W. Shepherd*

RIGHT: A cross-shaped pile of debris sits in the parking lot of Wal-Mart just hours after the tornado passed through Joplin. *Photo by B.W. Shepherd*

OPPOSITE: Carlye and Rance Junge pick through prescription bottles scattered throughout the wreckage of the Pronto Pharmacy on Maiden Lane. Rance rode out the storm inside the pharmacy. *Photo by Roger Nomer*

ABOVE: Employees walk through the 60,000-square-foot temporary store set up by Home Depot at 20th Street and Range Line. It was among a number of major employers to announce that they would rebuild in Joplin. *Photo by T. Rob Brown*

LEFT: Plumbers Bob Norris (left) and Darrell Harris, both with Mr. Rooter Plumbing, work at the site of a convenience store being rebuilt at the intersection of 20th Street and Duquesne Road. *Photo by T. Rob Brown*

BELOW: Large Caterpillar loaders work to remove rubble at the site of Home Depot on Range Line. Seven people perished when the tornado brought the building down. *Photo by B.W. Shepherd*

Chapter Four

OPERATION RISING EAGLE

JOPLIN HIGH SCHOOL WAS LEVELED, as was Franklin Technical Center. East Middle School – one of the Joplin School District's newest buildings – was a loss. Irving Elementary School was destroyed. And the list of buildings sustaining heavy damage included Cecil Floyd, Kelsey Norman, Duquesne and Eastmorland elementary schools, as well as the district's administration building.

Yet, two days after the May 22 tornado, school district officials made a bold announcement – school would start again as scheduled on Aug. 17.

Though faced with a situation that was never touched on in "superintendent school," Superintendent C.J. Huff said that it was the right call at the right time.

"We needed direction," he said. "We needed a goal. I know my team, and they will rise to any challenge you put in front of them. And what better challenge than to say that school will start on time?"

Not long after the tornado, the Joplin Board of Education approved a plan that was dubbed "Operation Rising Eagle."

Under the plan, 11th- and 12-graders would attend classes at the former Shopko building at Northpark Mall, while ninth- and 10th-graders would go to Memorial Education Center at Eighth Street and Wall Avenue. Franklin Technology Center programs would be housed in warehouse space at Fourth Street and Grand Avenue.

Finding space to house the high-school students was one of the most critical parts of the plan, said Huff, as it involved finding space for 2,200 students.

As it was just an open retail space, the Shopko building needed walls, lighting, ceilings and electricity. Huff said it was one of the most challenging projects the district faced, but one that held a lot of potential.

"That was a critical building for us to get," he said.

East Middle School students would have classes in a building at the Crossroads Business Center and Distribution Park. The fact that the school had been relatively new when it was hit by the tornado actually has an upside, said the superinentdent.

"We're going to rebuild it from the ground up," said Huff. "The designs are still there and we already have the floor plan."

Students from Irving were to attend the former Washington School at 1112 E. Second St.; Duquesne and Duenweg students would be housed at Duenweg Elementary; and Emerson students were to go to Duquesne. The administration offices were moved to the Missouri Department of Transportation building on 32nd Street, which allowed the renovated Roi S. Wood Administration Building to house the district's Beacon and Flex programs.

If it sounds like a lot like moving pieces around a game board, it's not far from the truth.

"I've been referring to it as a giant puzzle," said Huff. "You have to stop and think about what you have available and what the best fits are. We've been creative in how we approached it. Every time a puzzle piece shifted, it either helped us or hurt us as we gained or lost square footage and had to rearrange the puzzle again."

It's a plan that has had an effect on nearly every aspect of how the district operates, right down to the routes buses have to take to get students to their new locations.

But Huff said that there's no question that undertaking the ambitious plan was the right thing to do.

"You find out right away what kind of team you've got when you have an adversity like this," he

said. "To a person, they've all stepped up.

"School is not going to be exactly like it was last year, but we can rebuild buildings. What's important is to maintain the relationships that happen underneath those roofs … getting everyone back together so that the teaching and learning process can begin again."

Plans also came together to find a temporary home for the 210 students and 14 teachers from St. Mary's Elementary School, which was leveled by the tornado.

In June, officials with Joplin Area Catholic Schools announced that students would begin school on Sept. 6 in the former Simpson Sheet Metal building at 10th Street and Byers Avenue. The Springfield-Cape Girardeau Diocese already owned the building, which had been used by Catholic Charities for storage after the storm.

The Simpson building will not be a permanent home for the school, said St. Mary's Principal Steve Jones.

"We anticipate being out of it in a year or two, and (McAuley Catholic High School) could utilize it in various forms," he said. ∎

OPPOSITE: An aerial view shows the devastation at JHS. *Photo by Roger Nomer*

RIGHT: A member of the Joplin High School class of 2011 shows her excitement at being done with school during graduation on May 22. The ceremony ended shortly before the tornado touched down.
Photo by Roger Nomer

FAR RIGHT: Kelsee Shanks (left), of Carl Junction, hugs Theresa Adams, a preschool aid at St. Mary's School, in front of the school's wreckage after the tornado. *Photo by Roger Nomer*

BELOW: A view of the damage left in the tornado's path near Joplin High School. *Photo by T. Rob Brown*

LEFT: A memorial sits in front of St. Mary's Catholic Church and Elementary School. Students there were to begin the school year in the former Simpson Sheet Metal building, which is owned by the diocese.

Photo by T. Rob Brown

OPPOSITE TOP: Joplin High School was hit hard by the EF-5 tornado. It was among the Joplin School District properties declared a total loss. *Photo by B.W. Shepherd*

OPPOSITE BOTTOM: East Middle School was one of the most recent buildings constructed by the school district. Superintendent C.J. Huff said it will be rebuilt using the same plans. *Photo by B.W. Shepherd*

ABOVE: Joplin School District Superintendent C.J. Huff speaks outside the tornado-stricken Joplin High School. District officials decided that the 2011-12 school year would begin as scheduled. *Photo by T. Rob Brown*

OPPOSITE: Klista Reynolds (right), Joplin School District technology coordinator, and teacher Shelly Tarter comfort each other during an announcement about the future of the district. *Photo by T. Rob Brown*

Chapter Five

THE MEDICAL COMMUNITY

A LONGTIME RESIDENT OF JOPLIN, Horace Jackson wasn't alarmed when he heard the sound of sirens on May 22.

A patient at St. John's Regional Medical Center who was scheduled to be discharged the following day, he thought it was merely a precaution when hospital staff executed "Condition Gray" – moving patients and visitors out of hospital rooms and away from windows.

"They said, 'Mr. Jackson, we've got a tornado warning and we're going to move you into the hallway,'" he said.

He remembered sitting with dozens of other patients in that sixth-floor hallway.

Then Jackson said he heard a rumbling "like I was standing under a railroad trestle while a train was going over. I felt the building start to shake, and I heard things cracking and windows breaking."

Moments later, the hallway's double steel fire doors burst open, exposing Jackson to the full force of the EF-5 tornado's 200 mph winds, which moved the entire 367-bed, nine-story hospital off its foundation.

"When those doors ripped open, I've never felt anything that strong before in my life," he said. "It was like a 300-pound man running into you full blast. It was just horrific."

Jackson, who said he was the closest patient to the doors, squinted his eyes as rain and debris pelted him and others in the hallway. Wearing only a hospital gown and gripping a pillow, he said he was completely unprotected as debris battered his body. Flying debris struck him in the head. At that point, he got into the fetal position to try and protect himself. He was hit in the head a second time and said he could feel the wind pulling him. It was at that

moment he considered his own death.

"I really thought I was going to die," he said. "After I got hit in the head the second time and it was trying to pull me off the floor, I just said, 'God, if you're going to take me, take me fast. I don't want to be maimed or tore up. I just want to quickly die.' I guess He heard my prayers because I didn't die, but I felt like I was. I was as close to death as I want to experience."

In mid-July, Jackson passed away following a long illness.

At least nine people died at St. John's that night. Nurses and staff scrambled to assess the damage, and they were joined by nearby residents who helped to evacuate the 183 patients who were in the hospital.

Leslie Allen, a charge nurse in the emergency department at the nearby Freeman Hospital West, was near the end of her 12-hour shift on the evening of May 22.

She had started work at 6:15 a.m., spending her day coordinating and troubleshooting at the ER – making sure that staffing was adequate and that patients were getting to their assigned rooms.

Just after 5 p.m., about an hour before she was due to leave, the storm sirens went off.

"Our policy at the hospital is to get patients and visitors to safe areas," she said. "When the tornado watch was elevated to a warning, we moved them into interior rooms."

But it wasn't until the first person came into the hospital with injuries that Allen realized that Joplin had been hit by a tornado.

"Our first patient came in through the front door of the triage area," she said. "He was holding his intestines in his arms. He had been lacerated from one side of his body to the other.

"I said, 'My gosh, what happened?' And he said, 'It's the tornado. It's devastated everything.'"

That first patient was among those who did not survive.

As the severely injured and walking wounded began making their way to the hospital, Allen said she began noticing people already wearing hospital gowns. That was her first indication that St. John's had been hit. Within just the first few hours after the tornado, Freeman saw more than 500 patients who had sustained injuries in the tornado.

What struck Allen the most about that night was the sense of unity among Joplin's medical community.

"We had nurses and doctors from St. John's working side by side with us in the ER," she said. "There were doctors from Oklahoma and Arkansas here. I saw doctors who had quit their practices several years ago. There were specialists – plastic surgeons, dentists, anyone that had a skill to offer, they were here and offering it.

"There were no barriers. It was very comforting and exactly what we needed. It brought us all together as one unit."

In the weeks after the tornado, Freeman nearly doubled the volume of patients that it normally would see, said Allen.

"That Sunday morning when we clocked in, that would be our last day at Freeman as we knew it," she said.

OPPOSITE: Flanked by the damaged St. John's hospital, rescue workers and business owners search through the remains of a nearby building.

Photo by Mike Gullett

Temporary triage centers were also established at other locations, including Memorial Hall and Missouri Southern State University in the aftermath of the storm. Local patients were also transported to regional hospitals in Carthage, Neosho, Springfield, Pittsburg, Kan., Miami, Okla., and Tulsa, Okla.

Just one week later, St. John's celebrated the opening of a 60-bed field hospital in a parking lot within sight of their damaged building.

"It's been one week, and we're back," said Dottie Bringle, director of nursing. "That's so important to us, because we've been so supported by the community."

Gary Pulsipher, president and chief executive officer of the hospital, said that St. John's would rebuild and would keep all of its 1,800 employees on staff while it is being constructed. Because of their close proximity, he said that it was a miracle that Freeman was not affected by the tornado and that the new hospital would most likely not be built near its former location. ∎

ABOVE: St. John's is framed by the gas pump awnings at the Pronto Pharmacy on Maiden Lane.

Photo by Roger Nomer

RIGHT: Dr. C.A. Featherly, an emergency room doctor, discusses treatment options with Catherine Johnson at St. John's temporary hospital.

Photo by T. Rob Brown

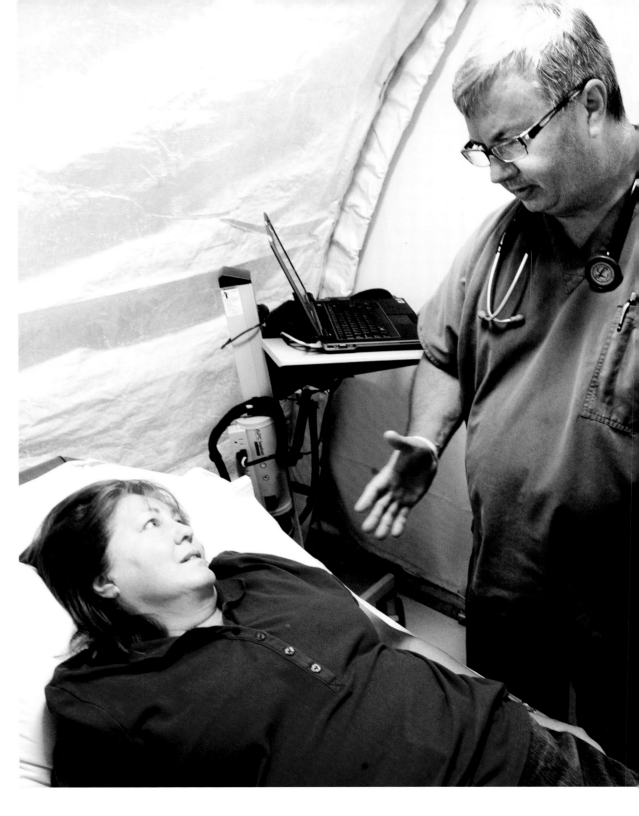

LEFT: Nurse Jessica Chorum pulls a bed into place inside St. John's temporary location. *Photo by Roger Nomer*

BELOW: The late Horace Jackson was among the patients at St. John's Regional Medical Center when the EF-5 tornado hit. *Photo by T. Rob Brown*

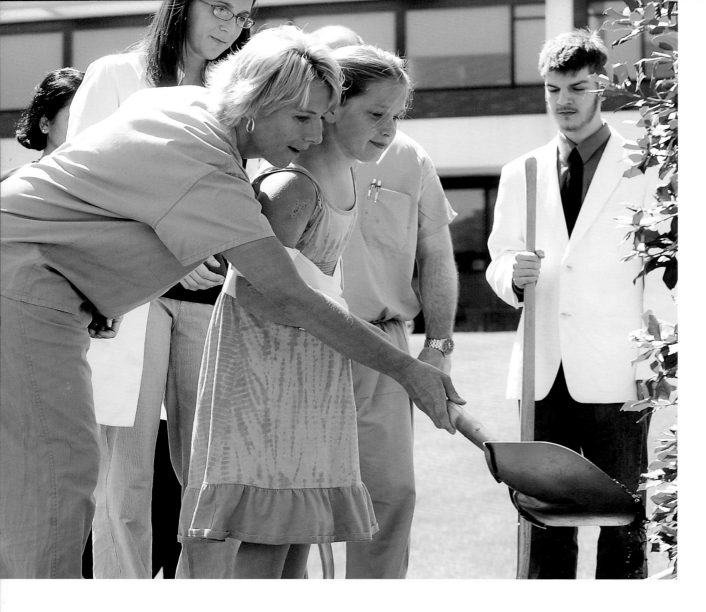

ABOVE: Sarah Allen, a physician's assistant, and Terri Walker, a cardiovascular scrub tech, help Mason Lillard plant a tree at Freeman Hospital. The two helped treat the young girl's injuries following the tornado.

Photo by Roger Nomer

RIGHT: One month after the May 22 tornado, Freeman Health System lit the night sky in order to pay tribute to the local healthcare workers who worked to save the lives of those injured in the storm.

Photo by Curtis Almeter

Chapter Six

JOPLIN'S PET PROJECT

PEOPLE WEREN'T THE ONLY ONES impacted by the May 22 tornado. In the aftermath of the storm, the Joplin Humane Society and the American Society for the Prevention of Animal Cruelty took in more than 1,300 displaced pets.

In the immediate days following the storm, pets without owners were taken to a makeshift shelter north of Joplin near the Animal Adoption and Resource Center. Pets with owners, but no homes, stayed with the rest of the displaced, in a shelter set up in the Leggett & Platt Athletic Center at Missouri Southern State University. The month following the storm turned the Humane Society and the area around it into what ASPCA workers began calling a "village." Warehouses were outfitted to comfortably house pets, while volunteers and workers lived in campers and trailers.

Over the weeks, a firm dirt path was worn through the grass between the pet warehouses and the Humane Society's main building. While cats and dogs made up the bulk of the homeless animals, the society also housed birds, goats, chickens, pigs, ferrets, rabbits, hermit crabs, snakes and even a fish – saved from its tank in a soon to be demolished apartment building by a rescue worker who scooped it up in a kitchen pot, put the lid on it and took it to the shelter.

The owner later came for the fish.

While approximately 500 lost pets were reunited with their owners, 700 healthy pets still remained more than a month after the storm.

The pets – spayed, neutered, microchipped and given current shots – were put up for adoption for free in a massive adopt-a-thon that drew people from 24 states.

"The reality is that homes have been destroyed and people have decided that the best thing is to allow their pets to go to loving homes," said Karen Aquino, executive director of the humane society's Animal Adoption and Resource Center.

The two-day adoption event, held in late June, saw more than 2,000 people lined up for hours in the sun to take home one of the "tornado pets." Gary Hallock, from Gallup, N.M., made the trip to Joplin to assist friends and ended up leaving with a small brown terrier-mix puppy, which he named Joplin.

Tim Rickey, senior director with the ASPCA, is originally from Joplin and has extensive experience in disaster zones. He said the Joplin tornado caused one of the highest numbers of displaced pets he had even seen. However, he also said he's seldom seen so many people come back to claim their animals, or such willingness to give the remaining animals new homes.

On July 1, the last of the displaced pets – 52 cats and kittens – were loaded into an airplane and flown to Seattle, Wash., where animal rescue groups would board them until they were ready to adopt. But the Joplin shelter didn't stay silent for long.

"In fact, when the shelter was empty, we could have put our feet up," Aquino said. "But we actually called other shelters that were overcrowded. We filled up our shelter the very next day." ∎

OPPOSITE: Brooke Hill, of Kansas City, Mo., kisses a brindle boxer-lab mix that she and her fiancé, Jesse Yoakum, were considering adopting at the Animal Adoption and Resource Center. *Photo by T. Rob Brown*

BELOW: People traveled to Joplin from 24 states to adopt a "tornado pet" at an adoption event held in June. *Photo by Curtis Almeter*

ABOVE: As cleanup gets under way in Duquesne, Abby Brewer shares a much needed drink with a dog named Miss Priss. *Photo by B.W. Shepherd*

ABOVE: Jean McNamara, of Portland, Ore., pets a lab/shepherd mix dog at the temporary animal shelter for pets displaced by the tornado. *Photo by Roger Nomer*

LEFT: Amber Curry and her son Alex are reunited with their family dog, Thunder. An entire "village" was created to house pets that were separated from their owners during the storm. *Photo by Curtis Almeter*

BELOW: Mike Scott, from Walnut Creek, Calif., takes a beagle mix dog for a walk at the temporary animal shelter near the Humane Society on North Main Street. *Photo by Roger Nomer*

RIGHT: Gena Berg, of Denver, helps load animals into a van that waited to take them to the airport to be flown to Seattle, where they would be housed by animal rescue groups. *Photo by Roger Nomer*

Chapter Seven
ROOTING FOR THE HOME TEAM

THE TORNADO STRUCK JOPLIN ON May 22 about 20 minutes after the St. Louis Cardinals beat the Kansas City Royals 9-8 in 10 innings in Kansas City.

One month later, the Cardinals and Royals played another three-game series in St. Louis, and Joplin was the center of attention as thousands of dollars were raised during the weekend to help with relief efforts.

"There's really no words to say," said Royals outfielder Jeff Francoeur, one of many major leaguers who has spent time in Joplin during USA Baseball activities. "You say you're sorry, we're doing all we can to raise money, but for those people who have been affected, it's never going to be the same."

"Teams Unite for Joplin" was the theme of the weekend series, and weekend activities – including $10 commemorative patches and auctions of VIP Cardinals experiences – raised more than $200,000.

The weekend also provided unforgettable experiences for some Joplin High School softball and baseball players.

Before the Friday night series opener, Mikaila Craig and Danielle Campbell – two softball players whose families lost their homes in the tornado – threw ceremonial first pitches.

For the second game, 18 Joplin High School baseball players went to Busch Stadium and stood behind home plate for part of batting practice. The Cardinals and Royals both wore Joplin High School baseball hats during batting practice. Then half of the Eagles took the field with the Cardinals in the top of the first inning, and the other nine went on the field with the Royals in the bottom of the first.

"It was a great experience, once-in-a-lifetime, being down on the field and get to interact with the players," said Tyler Meyer, who took the field with Royals first baseman Eric Hosmer. "It's amazing

how the support has come from around the country. We're on the map now. They know we're here, and they are willing to spend their time and help us and get us back on track."

The Joplin High School JROTC provided the color guard during pregame activities for the final game of the series.

The "Teams Unite for Joplin" theme actually could be applied to the entire recovery process as countless teams – professional, college and high school – sent donations or supplies to aid the victims.

The Kansas City Chiefs and St. Louis Rams made multiple trips to Joplin.

"Being part of a community and a state, it's all about giving back and making people smile," Rams offensive tackle Adam Goldberg said. "We're glad to bring them whatever happiness we can, whether it's having fun with the kids or shake some hands and try to lift some spirits.

"Whether it's signing an autograph for them, throwing the ball with them, playing Legos with them or giving them a pack of trading cards or just introducing them to the great Sam Bradford (Rams quarterback), we're just really happy to be here."

The Chiefs not only provided cleanup work on their second trip to Joplin, but they also gave autographs and posed for pictures with hundreds of fans.

Chiefs general manager Scott Pioli helped with cleanup on that trip and was surprised by the residents' reaction.

"They are thanking us for coming," he said. "Come on. It's the least we can do."

New Missouri Tigers basketball coach Frank Haith got the ball rolling for one unexpected athletic event. At his suggestion – and with the NCAA's approval –

the Tigers scheduled a men's basketball exhibition game against Missouri Southern in Joplin, the "One State, One Spirit Classic" presented by Leggett & Platt.

Missouri State, under new coach and former MSSU assistant Paul Lusk, also scheduled a game against the Lions in Joplin.

The University of Missouri was very active in relief efforts. The school sold thousands of T-shirts, "One State, One Spirit, One Mizzou, 5-22-11" online, and approximately 30 Tiger football players came down for an afternoon of work.

Oklahoma State allowed some Joplin High wrestlers to attend the Cowboys' summer camp free of charge, and the USTA orchestrated a $100,000 donation to help rebuild the tennis courts at the high school.

MCMURRAY'S OLD HOME

Before the NASCAR's first Sprint Cup race in June at Kansas Speedway, Joplin native Jamie McMurray came back home for a day.

He visited the Convoy of Hope, which was set up on a parking lot near Seventh Street and Maiden, Lane and toured the destruction area before going to his old home on East 25th Street that was brought down by the tornado.

"For me," McMurray said, "pulling into the

OPPOSITE: D.J. Williams (left) a Green Bay Packers draftee and an Arkansas Razorbacks alumnus, helps unload donations at McAuley Catholic High School. A group of about 60 Razorbacks came to help with tornado relief efforts. *Photo by T. Rob Brown*

neighborhood, you can't recognize anything … It's so hard to understand what you're looking at. Standing here looking, you know what it's supposed to look like, but it's just so different. Destroyed."

Actually, the door to McMurray's old bedroom helped save the lives of Donna and Thomas Tinker, who bought the home from Jamie's mother, Sue, four years earlier.

"I was in the hallway," Donna told Jamie. "I was in front of your door and Tom was laying on the floor in front of me. The hallway wall fell over on the other hallway wall, and we were underneath it.

"I was down on my knees. I really thought we were going to die. The door just protected us. It was one of the prettiest houses in the neighborhood.

"It was such a nice neighborhood. I just can't comprehend it all. It's just not real. But we're alive. I'm not complaining."

Seeing that his old home and old neighborhood had been blown away was not the hardest part of the day for McMurray.

"The most difficult part was the stories at the Convoy of Hope," he said. "I met some families,

ABOVE: NASCAR driver Jamie McMurray (right), who grew up in Joplin, listens to Aleta Whitely talk about the ordeal her granddaughter, Keana Caton, went through during the tornado. *Photo by T. Rob Brown*

and talking to some families who lost kids, that's the hardest part. To hear that story on TV from a news anchor interviewing, that's one thing, but to be with the person and hear it, it's a completely different feeling. I thought (seeing) my home would be the worst. I have emotional ties to that because I'll never see it again, but it's not even close."

JOPLIN LITTLE LEAGUE

Major League Baseball gave 12 Joplin Little League baseball players whose families lost their homes an unforgettable trip.

They went to Phoenix in early July to play in a Jr. RBI Classic tournament and then attend all the activities leading up to the All-Star Game.

After going 4-2 in the tournament wearing uniforms identical to the St. Louis Cardinals, the players visited the MLB Fanfest twice and attended the minor league Futures Game, the celebrity and legends softball game and the Home Run Derby. They also spent time with one of the all-stars, Justin Upton of the Arizona Diamondbacks.

"The whole thing is just awesome," said Alex Etter, one of the players. "Simply awesome." ■

ABOVE: Corbin Coucher, 8, of Joplin, gets his die-cast version of Jamie McMurray's Daytona win car signed by McMurray. During his visit to Joplin, McMurray spoke with residents impacted by the tornado and visited the house where he grew up, which was destroyed during the storm. *Photo by T. Rob Brown*

LEFT: During a visit to the shelter set up at the Leggett & Platt Athletic Center, Frank Haith, the new head basketball coach at Mizzou, shares a laugh with 2-year-old Alikai Haidle, whose home was destroyed by the tornado. Haith and his assistant coaches brought stuffed tigers to give to children and others in need of comfort. *Photo by T. Rob Brown*

RIGHT: Joplin High School softball players Danielle Campbell (left) and Mikaila Craig are all smiles as they walk out to the mound to throw out the ceremonial first pitches for the Kansas City Royals and St. Louis Cardinals baseball game on June 17 at Busch Stadium. *Photo by T. Rob Brown*

FAR RIGHT: A crowd of more than 40,000 baseball fans show their support for the St. Louis Cardinals, Kansas City Royals and Joplin as the two teams played on June 17 in St. Louis. The teams sponsored auctions during each game of the series to raise money for Joplin tornado relief. *Photo by T. Rob Brown*

BELOW: Kansas City's starting pitcher Filipe Paulino wears a Kansas City and St. Louis Teams Unite for Joplin patch during a baseball game. *Photo by T. Rob Brown*

Chapter Eight

HELPING HANDS

In the days and weeks after the tornado, thousands of men, women and children poured into Joplin from all points of the compass to help with the recovery efforts.

Dozens of high-school kids from just up the road in Miller. A church van full of volunteers from Muskogee, Okla. A bus of volunteers from Topeka, Kan. A caravan of 18 cars from a Methodist church near Chicago.

The list, the faces and the incoming vehicles went on and on ...

According to Lynn Onstot with the city of Joplin, volunteers through AmeriCorps and the United Way alone contributed nearly 70,000 hours during the three weeks after May 22.

"But this number represents just a fraction of the total outpouring of support from volunteers who have arrived in Joplin from around the country to serve through churches, civic groups and other local agencies," Onstot said.

Joplin officials, she continued, "would like to extend its heart-felt gratitude for everyone who has donated time, money or other resources to the recovery effort."

Almost two months after the tornado, the city announced that 53,836 registered volunteers had given 262,293 hours of their time toward recovery efforts.

QUICK RESPONSE

Relief efforts were quick to get under way.

Randy Gariss, pastor at College Heights Christian Church, said the recovery began almost immediately after the tornado tore through Joplin.

"It started coming together that evening," he said. "We have had hundreds of volunteers."

He said the church was coordinating with the city to help residents in need.

Volunteers were busy two days after the storm collecting, sorting, carrying and driving supplies to areas throughout Joplin.

Hallways of the church and school were filled with bottled water, paper towels, toiletries, bedding and children's toys. Tables in the gymnasium were piled high with donated clothing, and families made their way through with shopping carts as volunteers helped supply them with what they needed. Crates of bottled water were stacked 6 feet high in spots.

Across town, lines of trucks formed in front of The Bridge youth center as young volunteers filled them with clothes, food, medical supplies and bedding.

Dan Mitchell, director of the youth ministry, said social media sites such as Facebook helped get relief operations under way at the youth center. All of the center's staff members had been accounted for, he said.

About 150 volunteers were working the Tuesday after the tornado, and a few hundred more were expected to be pitching in by the end of the day, said Mitchell.

'I JUST NEED TO HELP'

At the parking lot at 15th Street and Virginia Avenue, helping unload truck trailers full of fruit drinks and Gatorade, Mike Coldren was a veteran of a 15-hour car ride. He drove from his home in a suburb of Pittsburgh, Penn., to Joplin in what amounted to an 889-mile haul.

When asked why he did what he did, a spur-of-the-moment kind of thing all by himself, Coldren simply shrugged his shoulders.

"To help," he said. "I watched this (disaster) from the very beginning. I just happened to be on vacation and I had nothing better to do."

Of what he had seen of the devastation left in the wake of the tornado, Coldren could only shake his head.

"TV just doesn't do it justice," he said. "It's pretty life-changing."

Trey Bean drove up from Hickory Creek, which lies on the shores of Beaver Lake between Rogers and Springdale in Northwest Arkansas, to help unload vehicles, trailers, vans and buses at The Bridge.

When asked why he decided to come, he just spread out his arms at the people rushing around and the cars waiting to unload and the piles of supplies beside him.

"This," he said. "As long as I've got the time, I'm here. And I'll come back."

Some of the volunteers chose to remain anonymous.

"It doesn't matter who I am," a Carthage man said when asked his name. "I just need to help. I just need to help. You see it on the TV all the time and you get a real eye-opener when it happens at home. I'm just trying to help any way I can."

AMERICORPS VOLUNTEERS

John Gomperts, the national director of AmeriCorps, came to town on June 5 to meet with

---

OPPOSITE : Salvation Army volunteer George Hugen, Kansas City, hands out a cold drink to Holden Holstein, 14, from Mount Vernon, as he works to clear debris. *Photo by Roger Nomer*

AmeriCorps members and with sailors from the USS Missouri working on a cleanup project in Joplin.

Gomperts said the first team of AmeriCorps members arrived in Joplin from St. Louis in the early morning after the night of the May 22 tornado. By the time of his visit, 130 or so AmeriCorps members were working in Joplin on the recovery.

AmeriCorps is part of the Corporation for National and Community Service, and is based in Washington, D.C. The government program allows people to volunteer for service to repay student loans. AmeriCorps members also receive a modest living allowance and health care coverage.

He said AmeriCorps members have served after other disasters – including Hurricane Katrina in New Orleans – but that did not prepare them for what they found in Joplin.

"That was awful, but this is stunning, shocking," Gomperts said. ■

TOP RIGHT: Parris Evans, of Diamond, calls to his rescue dog, Jody, as he searches for victims at the Greenbriar nursing home near 25th Street and Moffet Avenue. *Photo by Roger Nomer*

RIGHT: Kyle Saunder, with the Basehor (Kan.) Fire Department, searches for victims in the wreckage of a house near 26th Street. *Photo by Roger Nomer*

FAR RIGHT: Paul Cheatam carries Ian Ward away from the remains of a home to seek help after the tornado. *Photo by Mike Gullet*

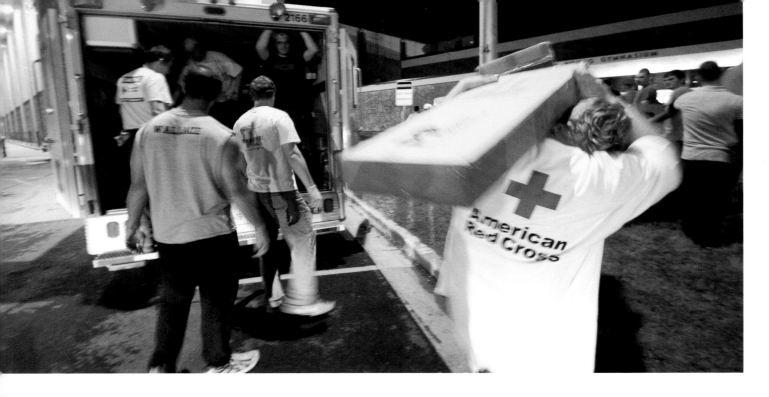

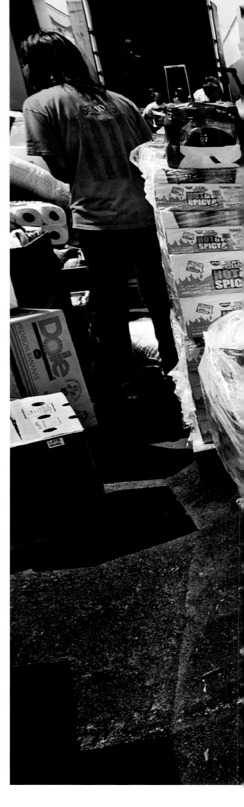

ABOVE: Volunteers and members of the Red Cross unload supplies from an ambulance into the MSSU gymnasium, which was temporarily being used as a shelter for tornado survivors. *Photo by Curtis Almeter*

RIGHT: Brandon Weaver, with Iron Mountain Assembly Church, unloads a van full of bottled water at College Heights Christian Church. *Photo by Curtis Almeter*

FAR RIGHT: Kimberly Ward (right), a Central Christian Center church member who lost her apartment in the tornado, helps unload a group of tractor trailers. *Photo by T. Rob Brown*

ABOVE: Bethany Hale, with the National Weather Service and National Oceanic Atmospheric Administration, looks at some of the damage left in the wake of the EF-5 tornado on Iowa Avenue, near Joplin High School. *Photo by T. Rob Brown*

LEFT: Kristen Killgore, a volunteer from Vicksburg, Miss., works with Samaritan's Purse International Relief to remove tornado debris. *Photo by T. Rob Brown*

OPPOSITE: Lamar residents Aaron Finney (center), Kieran Hanley (right) and Trevor Hobbs (left) get some help from Missouri State Rep. Mike Kelley as they move the remains of a porch to a debris pile near 23rd Street and Kentucky Avenue. Kelley was among a group of 30 legislators who came to Joplin to help with cleanup efforts.

Photo by T. Rob Brown

ABOVE: (From left) Crystal Garcia, from Midwest City, Okla.; Jessica Belle, of Oklahoma City, Okla.; and Tony Gordon, of St. Louis, load a wheelbarrow with storm debris at Sunny Jim Park. *Photo by Roger Nomer*

RIGHT: A message of thanks greets a group of volunteers from Tennessee who came to lend their help in Joplin. *Photo by Mike Gullett*

ABOVE: Travis Fitzgerald (left), of Manituwoc, Wis., and Ryan Sullivan, Chicago, Ill., both from the USS Missouri, clean up debris near St. John's. *Photo by Roger Nomer*

OPPOSITE: AmeriCorps volunteer Doyle Herrin, Pineville, shovels tornado debris at a site near Joplin High School. *Photo by Roger Nomer*

RIGHT: Glen Hogh, owner of Vega restaurant of Metairie, La., cooks up some crayfish pasta in Landreth Park. *Photo by T. Rob Brown*

86

LEFT: Amber Watkins sorts through stacks of donated clothes for her 4-year-old niece, whose house was destroyed by the tornado. *Photo by Curtis Almeter*

BELOW: Terrell Kabal, 9, helps to sort through clothes inside the old New York & Company store inside Northpark Mall. *Photo by Curtis Almeter*

ABOVE: U.S. Secretary of Homeland Security Janet Napolitano, flanked by law-enforcement representatives, speaks to the media in front of the Donald Clark Law Enforcement and Public Safety Building during a visit on June 9. *Photo by T. Rob Brown*

LEFT: Pastor William Pape delivers a sermon in front of the remains of Peace Lutheran Church. Many Joplin churches destroyed or damaged by the tornado held services outside or found an alternate location to gather. *Photo by Roger Nomer*

Chapter Nine

DEATH DOES NOT GET THE LAST WORD

My family lives south of town and after the tornado I drove as far as I could into town and then ran to the home of one of my closest friends – his house was gone, but he was safe.

From there I ran to the church and found about a third of it gone. I had to know if anybody was inside. One volunteer was in the kitchen and she was safe. I went out to the street and people were running. I didn't know what else to do so I just ran alongside people and said, "Can I help you find somebody?" I dug through houses, I prayed with a young couple who found friends who didn't make it out. Across the street an elderly couple lay dead in the backyard. Running, digging, hoping, praying.

I got called back to the church. The kids' wing of our church was miraculously still standing and it became a triage center. Classrooms – where, that morning children played and laughed and learned about Jesus – became places where the wounded were being treated, broken bones were being set, emergency surgeries were performed. Tables – where kids had been making crafts a few hours earlier – became beds and places of comfort and rest for the wounded.

We have all spent the last seven days looking for our family and friends. We've all had those moments of unbelievable relief at hearing somebody's voice. We have all had that moment of heart-sinking pain at hearing that someone we know didn't make it. Late Friday night I delivered the news to Mark and Trish Norton that their son Will's body had been identified. Eighteen years old and absolutely overflowing with life and faith. He had just graduated from high school before he was killed.

Will is one of 162. The word of comfort today for Will's family and for all the grieving comes from

the God of the universe who took human form and walked this earth. He suffered and knows what it's like when we do. Jesus said: "Do not let your hearts be troubled. Trust in God; trust also in me. In my Father's house are many rooms; if it were not so, I would have told you. I am going there to prepare a place for you. And if I go and prepare a place for you, I will come back and take you to be with me that you also may be where I am. Before long, the world will not see me anymore, but you will see me. Because I live, you also will live.

"Peace I leave with you; my peace I give you. I do not give to you as the world gives. Do not let your hearts be troubled and do not be afraid" (John 14:1-3, 19, 27, NIV).

To the families of those who died, God is saying to you right now, "Death does not get the last word. That's what I wanted you to see in Jesus' resurrection. Death doesn't win. Even when you think it does, it does not. Life wins."

I don't know the faith stories of all those who have died, but I do know this, God's grace is wider than we can imagine, and that heaven is real, and that this life is not the only life.

Some of us are asking why God did this or allowed it. So much death and destruction. But Jesus never promised that we would be protected from the storms of life. He never promised that life would be easy or convenient if we chose to follow him – almost all of his disciples were tortured to death. What he did promise was to be with us. To be with us through the storm. To be with us as we grieve. To be with us as we stand at the graveside of our loved ones. To be with us and listen to us and guide us. Our challenge is to let him. As hard as it may be, pray, talk to God, listen for his words. Let him love you.

Listen, God didn't do this to Joplin to punish us. Read the book. Jesus took our punishment for us. This happened because life on this side of eternity is unpredictable, chaotic and broken. But the scripture says, "For God so loved the world that he gave his one and only Son …" And he hasn't stopped loving the world. You may wonder at times, but the fact is God loves you, God loves Joplin, and God is walking with us through this tragedy and he will make a way where it seems there is no way.

You know, when Jesus was crucified everybody, and I mean everybody, thought that it was the end. The disciples had forgotten what he told them, their world had come crashing down, and eerie darkness covered the land. And for parts of three days there was no hope. But then, but then, but then Easter. Death is swallowed up in victory! Light crushes the darkness. Life wins.

Life won then. Life wins now. And now we get busy. Jesus didn't come back from the grave just to point us to heaven. He came back from the grave to give us a mission. That those who call on his name would be a light to the world. His mission is for us to get busy living. Get busy serving. Get busy rebuilding our city – which I love and believe is the center of the universe. Get busy loving more deeply than you ever have. Get busy taking care of your soul and connecting to the God who knows you by name and loves you more than you can imagine or believe.

For those of you who have lost loved ones, get

OPPOSITE: Rev. Aaron Brown shares a message of faith during trying times at the community memorial service on May 29. *Photo by B.W. Shepherd*

busy living out their legacy. They may have lost their lives, but none of them would want you to stop living yours because they're gone. Get busy living.

We are not a people without hope, we are people from whom hope, life, and light will shine to the ends of the earth. Because God is good all the time, and all the time God is good. And in the name of Jesus, Lord of life, and light, and hope and new beginnings, that is the Good News. ■

By Rev. Aaron Brown

Rev. Aaron Brown is the lead pastor at Saint Paul's United Methodist Church. He was among the speakers during the May 29 community memorial service held in Taylor Performing Arts Center at Missouri Southern State University.

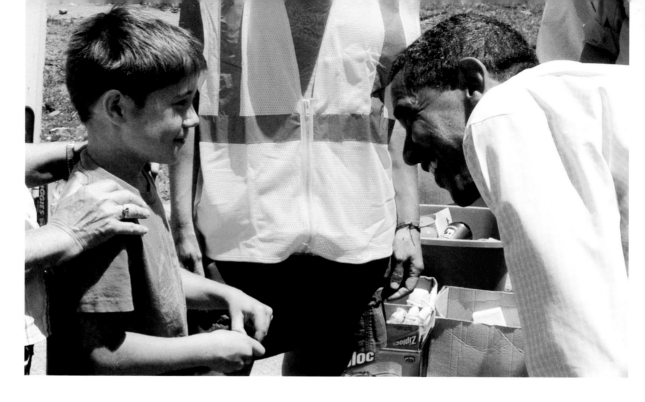

ABOVE: Area residents show their pride with flags and signs as the president's motorcade travels to Missouri Southern for the memorial service.

Photo by Curtis Almeter

OPPOSITE TOP: President Barack Obama stops to speak with Tanner Hills as he visits with families impacted by the tornado during a tour of the area near Joplin High School. *Photo by T. Rob Brown*

OPPOSITE BOTTOM: President Obama tours an area hit hard by the May 22 tornado. *Photo by T. Rob Brown*

93

ABOVE: A group displays their pride in Joplin at the corner of Range Line and Newman Road. In the hours before the memorial service on May 29, thousands of people gathered to honor the town as a counter protest to an expected visit by an extremist group.

Photo by B.W. Shepherd

RIGHT: A man who showed up to protest at the memorial service for the Joplin tornado victims is escorted away by police for his own safety.

Photo by Curtis Almeter

LEFT: President Barack Obama speaks to those gathered for the community memorial service in Taylor Performing Arts Center at Missouri Southern State University. *Photo by T. Rob Brown*

BELOW: Torrie Epperson, of Joplin, holds close her 5-week-old baby, Alice, as she waits for the start of the memorial service at Missouri Southern State University. *Photo by T. Rob Brown*

ABOVE: Sisters Kathy White (left) and JoAnn Molinas share an embrace during the moment of silence held at 5:41 p.m. on May 29 – one week after the tornado. *Photo by Curtis Almeter*

LEFT: Sam Nguyen says a prayer as he and Christina Perry observe a moment of silence at Cunningham Park. *Photo by Roger Nomer*

FAR LEFT: Missouri Gov. Jay Nixon gestures as he speaks during the memorial service in Taylor Performing Arts Center. *Photo by T. Rob Brown*

Chapter Ten

FACES OF THE STORM

AMONG THEIR RANKS ARE 18-YEAR-OLD Will Norton, an aspiring filmmaker returning home from his graduation ceremony when he became one of the first casualties of the May 22 tornado; and J.T. Strickland, 85, a veteran of WWII who passed away on July 8 from injuries sustained as the storm cut a deadly path through town.

Between are reminders that the tornado held little mercy for those caught in its path – from 16-month-old Skyuler Logsdon, torn from his mother's arms; to Lorie and Glenn Holland, who had just returned to Joplin from celebrating their wedding anniversary. Their ranks include students and retirees, veterans and homemakers, fathers and mothers, sons and daughters.

One hundred and sixty people – whose lives, in most cases, had likely never intersected before that day – connected by tragedy, forever linked together as the faces of the storm. ■

José O. Alvarez, 59, of Joplin, was an assistant professor of Spanish at Missouri Southern State University for the past three years. Originally from Colombia, he previously taught at Florida International University in Miami, where he had earned his doctoral degree in Spanish and served as a writer and editor for the Univision television network.

Maria L. Alvarez-Torres, 43, of Joplin, was born in Mexico, where most of her family lives. She was the mother of five sons. Her boyfriend, Miguel Vasquez-Castillo, also died in the tornado.

Sarah Lee Anderson, 46, of Joplin, spent the past 10 years as a secretary at Joplin South Middle School. She was a member of the Joplin Church of Christ. Her husband, William, died with her in the storm. She is survived by her daughter, Grace, and her son, Quinton.

William Austin Anderson, 53, of Joplin, was employed for 30 years by Office Concepts and was a member of the Joplin Church of Christ. His wife, Sarah, died with him in the storm. He is survived by his daughter, Grace, and his son, Quinton.

Grace Aquino, 46, of Joplin, worked as a hostess for the China Pantry. She was at her church, Harmony Heights Baptist, with her family when the tornado hit. She threw herself over her 12-year-old son, Malachi, who survived. She is also survived by her husband, Rizaldy Aquino, whom she married in 1986 in the Philippines, and two daughters, Divine Aquino and Eunice Aquino.

Cyrus Edward Ash Jr., 87, of Joplin, was a U.S. Navy veteran of World War II who formerly worked at the receiving department of Lozier. A member of College Heights Christian Church, he was an expert billiards player and fished at Shoal Creek nearly every evening. He was a married father with two daughters, a grandfather of four and a great-grandfather of five.

Bruce M. Baillie, 56, of Joplin, was a page designer for The Joplin Globe and the father of a college-age daughter. Born in British Columbia, he worked for several Canadian newspapers before buying a bed-and-breakfast in Sedona, Ariz. He later worked for the Benton County (Arkansas) Daily Record and joined the Globe in 2003.

Robert W. Baker, 54, of Joplin, was a married father with two daughters and four grandchildren. He worked at the parts desk at Cycle Connection.

Robert E. Bateson Jr., 47, of Joplin, was a licensed master plumber and an employee of Modine Manufacturing Co. He was a lifelong resident of Joplin and a member of Central Christian Center. He was also a father of three and grandfather of three.

Lathe Edward Bradfield, 84, of Joplin, was a World War II Army veteran, a Purple Heart recipient, an auto mechanic and a member of the Teamsters union. He worked on cars every day, whether it was at work or at home. Survivors include his wife, two daughters, one son and two grandchildren.

Ramona M. Bridgeford, 77, of Seneca, formerly taught preschool in California and was a member of Harmony Heights Baptist Church. She was a mother and grandmother.

Leo E. Brown, 86, of Joplin, was a retired clergyman of the Christian Church (Disciples of Christ) who was a patient at St. John's Regional Medical Center when the tornado struck. Survivors include his wife, a son, a daughter, two grandchildren and one great-grandchild.

Hugh Odell Buttram, 85, of Joplin, was a veteran of World War II and a salesman for more than 50 years in the insurance business. He was married to Evelyn Buttram.

Tami L. Campbell, 28, of Joplin, formerly of Watertown, Wis., was employed in Joplin at Wal-Mart as a photo lab technician. She was a member of St. Mark's Evangelical Lutheran Church. She loved photography and tigers. Survivors include her husband, Steven, two sons, Jordan and Caleb, and a stepson, Austin Powell.

Arriyinnah Carmona, 8, of Joplin, was a second-grade student at Royal Heights Elementary School. Her father, Moises Carmona, died with her in the storm. Survivors include her mother, Kari, and two sisters, Marisela and Adriennah.

Moises Carmona, 42, of Joplin, was born in Mexico and moved here from Albuquerque, N.M., in 2001. He was a heavy equipment operator for Anchor Stone Co. and a member of the Joplin Full Gospel Church. He was the married father of three daughters, one of whom died with him in the storm.

Shante Marie Caton, 10, of Joplin, was a student at Eastmorland Elementary School. She is survived by her parents, Moses Caton and Crystal Whitely, and one sister, Keana Caton.

Trentan Maurice Steven Caton, 6, of Joplin, was a student at Eastmorland Elementary School. He is survived by his parents, Moses Caton and Crystal Whitely, and one sister, Keana Caton.

Raymond LeRoy Chew Sr., 66, of Joplin, was a heavy equipment operator who had worked for the Webb City Special Road District. He was a U.S. Marine Corps veteran and a member of Cornerstone Church in Carterville. He was a married father with two sons, a daughter, 11 grandchildren and two great-grandchildren.

Clyde Coleman, 72, of Galena, Kan., was the former owner and operator of Coleman's Upholstery Shop in Galena. He also worked for USD 499 as a bus monitor and crossing guard. He was a 35-year member of the Joplin Elks Lodge and enjoyed reading, gardening, storytelling and doing community service. He is survived by his wife, two daughters, five grandchildren and six great-grandchildren.

Carolane Jean Collins, 62, of Eagle Rock, was a retired quality control technician for EaglePicher Technologies. She belonged to the Lighthouse Pentecostal Church and enjoyed cooking, spending time with her family, canning and looking for antiques. Survivors include her husband, a daughter, five grandchildren and one great-grandchild.

Lois Ada Comfort, 66, of Webb City, was a longtime employee of EaglePicher. She enjoyed fishing and working in her yard. Survivors include her husband of nearly 20 years, two sons, a daughter and six grandchildren.

Keenan Krise Conger, 49, of Carl Junction, gave his life trying to protect his two dogs, Sissy and Sally, who both survived the storm. He worked at a Minnesota boatyard in his youth and enjoyed working on motorbikes.

James V. Cookerly, 49, of Joplin, worked in the heating and air-conditioning field. He moved to Joplin a year ago from McDonald County. Survivors include his wife, two children and three grandchildren.

Teddy Ray Copher, 71, of Joplin, was an employee of TAMKO Building Products for 31 years. He is survived by one son, Richard Copher, and six grandchildren.

Malisa Ann Crossley, 36, of Joplin, was an employee of the Wal-Mart store on Seventh Street for two years. She was described by her family as a loving mother, and she protected her 9-year-old son during the tornado. Survivors include two sons and one daughter.

Adam D. Darnaby, 27, of Joplin, was an electrician for Jasper Products. He attended the House of Prayer and the Riverton Friends Church. His interests included the outdoors, fast cars, racing and four-wheeling. He is survived by his wife, parents and two brothers.

Patricia Dawson, 74, of Joplin, was a homemaker and member of the Temple Baptist Church in Springfield. Survivors include three sons, three grandchildren and one great-grandchild.

Nancy Elizabeth Douthitt, 94, of Joplin, was the owner of Douthitt Grocery Store on North Gray Avenue in Joplin until 1987. She was also a member of St. Paul's United Methodist Church. Survivors include one son, three grandchildren and eight great-grandchildren.

Ellen Jeanette Doyle, 75, of Joplin, was a homemaker and member of College Heights Christian Church. She loved to spend time with her family, eat out at restaurants and shop. Survivors include two daughters, five grandchildren and five great-grandchildren.

Faith Constance Dunn, 71, of Joplin, was a graduate of Ozark Christian College, where she worked for almost 20 years in the music department. She also taught sign language and was an avid horseman, riding with two separate drill teams. She was a member of the Park Plaza Christian Church.

Amonda Sue (Brashear) Eastwood, 49, of Joplin, was a registered nurse and was employed at Freeman Health System for several years. She was the mother of one son and two daughters, and had three grandchildren.

Richard Allen Elmore, 70, of Joplin, was a resident of the Greenbriar nursing home and a retired foreman of a Tulsa, Okla., steel company. He loved his church, Saginaw Baptist Church, and is survived by his wife, five sons, five grandchildren and one great-grandchild.

Randy Edward England, 34, of Granby, was an employee of La-Z-Boy in Neosho. He enjoyed barbecuing, watching movies, playing "Rock Band," reading and playing golf. He recently had planned a family trip to Texas to go deep-sea fishing. He is survived by his wife, Kelly, and two children, Julie, 12, and Justin, 8.

Betty Jo Burrington Fisher, 86, of Joplin, was the owner of Betty's Beauty Shop for many years. She was a member of Blendville Christian Church and was a 4-H leader. She also volunteered at St. John's Regional Medical Center and enjoyed square-dancing. Survivors include three daughters, one son, eight grandchildren, 10 great-grandchildren and one great-great-grandchild.

Robert S. Fitzgerald, 61, of Joplin, was a U.S. Army veteran from the Vietnam War, a St. Louis Cardinals fan, a 27-year employee of Wal-Mart and a 10-year cancer survivor. He loved collecting music, reading and playing Santa Claus to his nieces and nephews. He is survived by his wife of 33 years, Marti Fitzgerald.

Charles Kenneth Gaudsmith, 21, of Carthage, was a cook at the McDonald's restaurant on the south side of Carthage, and a former Carthage High School football player and wrestler. Survivors include his father and a sister. His mother, Melissa Renee Johnson, died with him in the storm.

Billie Jo Gideon, 77, of Joplin, worked for 32 years at the Pentecostal Church of God headquarters and Messenger Publishing. She attended the First Pentecostal Church of God, now known as Crown of Life Chapel. She was previously married to Delbert Gideon and had three sons, two daughters, 12 grandchildren and 24 great-grandchildren.

Robert M. Griffin, 61, of Battlefield, worked for Wickman's Garden Village for more than 18 years. He loved restoring old cars, particularly Mustangs. He is survived by his wife, Kay, his daughter, Bobbi Magana, and two grandchildren.

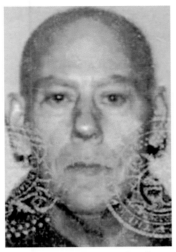

Paul E. "Gene" Haddock Sr., 62, of Joplin, worked as a welder for Lozier for 25 years before retiring. He was well known at the Joplin Family Y. Survivors include his wife, Karen, three sons and two grandchildren.

Johnna Hale, 49, of Joplin, worked for FAG Bearing Co. She loved Westerns, with "City Slickers" being her favorite movie, and dreamed of visiting the Redwood forest in California and driving Highway 1. She loved animals and was found after the tornado with her dog, Star, in her arms. Survivors include her children.

Leola L. (McCune) Hardin, 76, of Joplin, retired in 2000 as a packer for Bagcraft. She also made lap blankets for Hospice Compassus. Survivors include two sons, one daughter and three grandchildren.

Caley Lantz Hare, 16, of Joplin, had lived in Joplin since 1998 and was a straight-A student in the junior class at Joplin High School. He was an avid BMX bike rider, and he volunteered at The Bridge and Autumn Ramp Park. He attended Christ's Church of Joplin. He is survived by his mother, father, one brother and two sisters.

Dorothy Viola Hartman, 91, of Joplin, was a homemaker and member of the Bethel Methodist Church. She is survived by her husband of 70 years, a daughter, two grandchildren, three great-grandchildren and three great-great-grandchildren.

Dee Ann Hayward, 47, of Galena, Kan., worked for Hallmark Cards and loved music. She was a Sunday school teacher at Riverton Friends Church and had traveled to Brazil and Jamaica as a missionary. She was married to Jim Hayward and had two sons and a daughter.

Glenn Wayne Holland, 59, of Joplin, was a retired veteran of the U.S. Air Force and an employee of Leggett & Platt. He was a member of the Retired Military Officers Association, the National Rifle Association and the American Legion. He and his wife, Lorie, who died with him in the storm, had just celebrated their 15th wedding anniversary at Walt Disney World.

Lorie Marie Holland, 48, of Joplin, had most recently worked at Allgeier, Martin & Associates. She loved scrapbooking and had been training for the Boomtown Days half marathon. She was a seasonal worker at Ozark Christian College and also worked the polls on election day. Her husband, Glenn, died with her in the storm.

Harli Jayce Howard, 5, of Joplin, was the daughter of Russell Howard, who also died in the tornado. She was found in her father's arms. She loved to talk and was known as the family chatterbug. She is survived by her mother, Edie Howard.

Hayze Cole Howard, 19 months, of Joplin, was the son of Russell Howard, who also died in the tornado. He was found in his father's arms. He is survived by his mother, Edie Howard.

Russell T. "Rusty" Howard, 29, of Joplin, was an electrician for PCS Phosphates and a member of the Kansas Army National Guard. He enjoyed fishing and riding motorcycles. His two children, Harli and Hayze, were found in his arms after the tornado. He is survived by his wife, Edie Howard.

Wendy Ann Istas, 58, of Joplin, was co-owner and operator of J-W Solutions with her husband, Jason Istas. She was also a Quick Books instructor at Franklin Technology Center and a director for the Stained Glass Theatre. She enjoyed sewing, doing crafts and spending time with her grandchildren. She is survived by her husband, four children and 10 grandchildren.

Jane E. Jaynes, 86, of Joplin, owned and operated Gene's Dari Jane at 26th and Main streets in Joplin with her husband, Eugene, who preceded her in death in 1998. She was a member of Joplin Heights Baptist Church. Survivors include one son, one daughter, four grandchildren and three great-grandchildren.

Melissa Renee Johnson, 50, of Carthage, was a homemaker, mother of two sons and a daughter, and grandmother of three. She was preceded in death by both sons, including one, Charles Gaudsmith, who also died in the tornado.

Cheryl L. Jones, 39, of Altamont, Kan., was a patient at St. John's Regional Medical Center when the tornado struck. A 1989 graduate of Independence Bible School, she worked as a telemetry technician at Via Christi St. Francis Hospital in Wichita, Kan., for several years. She enjoyed playing the piano and writing in her journal. She is survived by her son, Brendan Hamilton.

Kathy Keling, 53, of Joplin, had a son, a daughter and five grandchildren. Her family said she was a beautiful, nurturing caregiver. She was a member of Glendale Christian Church and Southland Christian Church in Springfield.

James "David" Kendrick, 63, of Joplin, was a U.S. Army veteran of the Vietnam War. He retired after 40 years with what formerly was Atlas Powder Co. He loved to fish and to tell his stories of prospecting for gold in Alaska. He was active in the Elks Club and the Gold Prospecting Association of America. Survivors include his daughter and grandson.

Abraham H. Khoury, 26, of Joplin, was a 2004 graduate of Joplin High School and was pursuing a degree in business and entrepreneurship at Missouri Southern State University. He worked as a server at Outback Steakhouse and loved fishing, camping, Texas Hold 'Em poker, football and the Kansas City Chiefs. Survivors include his mother, father, three brothers and a sister.

Stanley Dale Kirk, 62, of Joplin, was an aircraft engine technician for 38 years with Rocketdyne, Teledyne, Sabreliner and Premier Turbines. He was also a member of the National Guard and United Aerospace Workers. Survivors include his wife, Janice, his daughter, Jodelle, and his son, Bobby Giger Jr.

Geneva Eutsler Koler, 84, of Joplin, was a resident of the Greenbriar nursing home. She was a lifelong area resident who had worked for La-Z-Boy in Neosho. She is survived by two sons, two grandchildren and five great-grandchildren.

Donald Wayne Lansaw Jr., 31, of Joplin, owned a machine shop and was a licensed real estate agent with Charles Burt. He loved being outdoors and especially enjoyed camping and going on float trips. He is survived by his wife, Bethany, whom he shielded with his body when the tornado hit their Joplin home.

Bruce Allen Lievens, 48, of Joplin, was an avid sports fan and lover of antiques. He worked for Circle L Auction Service for more than 30 years. He also loved being with his family, which included his parents, four siblings and 13 nieces and nephews.

Skyuler Ignatius Logsdon, 16 months, of Joplin, was the son of Corderro I. Logsdon and Carol J. Tate.

Christopher Don Lucas, 27, a former resident of Vinita, Okla., was the assistant manager of the Pizza Hut on Range Line Road in Joplin. He served his country in the U.S. Navy for six years. He was the father of two daughters, Chloe Lucas and Emily Lucas, and was expecting a third child.

Patricia Mann, 64, of Joplin, worked for Rouse Heating and Air Conditioning for about 25 years. She loved animals and enjoyed reading, particularly mystery novels. Survivors include a brother.

Jesse Len McKee, 44, of Neosho, was a U.S. Air Force veteran, a self-employed master electrician and a member of Set Free Ministries in Wyandotte, Okla. He was an avid fisherman, hunter and musician. Survivors include his wife and three children.

James Edward McKeel, 69, of Joplin, was a baker for more than 30 years for several companies in the Joplin area. He loved to entertain and cook for his family. He is survived by two sons, two daughters, seven grandchildren and five great-grandchildren. His wife, Mary, died with him during the storm.

LaDonna S. McPurdy, 68, of Joplin, grew up in Parsons, Kan., and taught cosmetology classes at Vatterott College in Joplin. She was also a hair stylist in Parsons before moving to Missouri. She enjoyed painting, ceramics, gardening, fishing and traveling. Survivors include her husband, one son, four daughters, 27 grandchildren and 28 great-grandchildren.

Randall Elvin Mell, 49, of Webb City, was a Lionbacker and a custodian at the Jasper County Courthouse in Carthage. He loved Webb City sporting events and productions at local theaters. He attended Open Door Baptist Church in Carthage. Survivors include his parents and sister.

Angelina Ann Menapace, 52, of Joplin, worked as an office manager for Behavior Management Associates for 12 years. She enjoyed cooking, shopping and playing with her Boston terrier, Frank Duke. She also loved to prepare big meals for her family during the Thanksgiving and Christmas seasons. She is survived by two children and two granddaughters.

Ray Donald "Tripp" Miller III, 49, of Joplin, worked at Joplin Workshops. He was called "No. 1 Uncle" by his nieces and nephews, and he was a fan of the St. Louis Cardinals and University of Missouri sports. His friends and roommates, Rick Fox and Mark Farmer, died with him in the storm. Survivors include his parents and siblings.

Edith "Edie" L. Moore, 48, of Joplin, was raised in Columbus, Kan., and spent the past several years in Joplin. She was a dedicated mother of a son, Bowen Greninger, and a daughter, Emily DeGraff, and loved her adopted cats.

Georgia "Nadine" Mulkey, 91, of Joplin, had worked in school food service and at Sale Memorial Hospital, now Freeman Neosho Hospital. She attended First Baptist Church in Neosho and is survived by four children, five grandchildren and six great-grandchildren.

Edmund Vincent Mullaney, 82, of Joplin, was a resident of the Greenbriar nursing home. He was a veteran of the U.S. Marine Corps and a member of Our Lady of the Lake Catholic Church and the Knights of Columbus. Survivors include his wife, Marilyn.

Sharyl Anyssa Nelsen, 34, of Webb City, was working as a sales representative for the AT&T store on Range Line Road and helped guide a family out of danger before the tornado struck. She is survived by her husband, Chad, and her children, Matilyn, Aaron and Ashley.

William Richard Norton, 18, of Joplin, graduated from Joplin High School on the day of the tornado. He loved to travel and had recently become a private pilot. He played tennis and was part of the high school's nationally recognized Constitution Team. He planned to attend Chapman University and major in film production. He is survived by his parents and his sister.

Dennis M. Osborn, 34, of Seneca, worked for Jasper Products and was a member of the 203rd National Guard, having served his country during the Iraq War. He is survived by his wife, Steffannie, one son, Matthew, and one daughter, Aundrea.

Charles E. Oster, 77, of Joplin, was a veteran of the Korean War and a semi-retired salesman for Share Corp. of Milwaukee, Wis. He served as a deacon at the First Christian Church in Webb City. He is survived by his wife, two sons, one daughter, five grandchildren and 10 great-grandchildren. His daughter, Loretta Randall, also died in the tornado.

Shirley Ann Parker, 68, of Joplin, was a mammography technician, retired from the Loveless Health Care System in Albuquerque, N.M. Survivors include a son, Greg Parker, a daughter, Stephanie Woods, and six grandchildren.

Nichole Sherie Pearish, 23, of Joplin, was active in Future Farmers of America before graduating from Sarcoxie High School in 2006. She worked as a customer service supervisor at Aegis Communications and was a member of the First Baptist Church of Sarcoxie and the Route 66 Cloggers. She is survived by her parents, six brothers and one sister.

James Benjamin John Peterson, 27, of Joplin, was a 2003 graduate of Joplin High School and an employee of the McDonald's restaurant on Main Street. He is survived by his mother, stepfather and sister.

John Henry "Jay" Petty Jr., 37, of Joplin, was a former U.S. Army Ranger who spent the past five years working at Jasper Products. He loved to hunt, fish and play the guitar with his band, Iris Road. Survivors include his fiancee and two daughters, Hannah Petty and Hayli Petty.

Hallie "Marie" Cook Piquard, 78, of Joplin, was a former deputy collector for Jasper County and a former employee of Contract Freighters Inc. A member of Harmony Heights Baptist Church, she enjoyed bowling and Southern gospel music. Survivors include two sons, three daughters, 13 grandchildren and 24 great-grandchildren.

Natalia Puebla, 17, of Carthage, had just completed her first year at Ozark Christian College. She was a member of the Joplin Full Gospel Church and was loved by her piano students, church family and college friends. She is survived by her parents, two brothers and one sister. Her aunt, Sandra Thomas, also died in the storm.

Shelly Marie Ramsey, 42, of Neosho, was the mother of one son and one daughter. She was described by her family as very giving and always having a smile and positive attitude. She worked at Jay Hatfield Mobility in Joplin.

Lorretta Lea Randall, 54, of Webb City, taught at the SEK Learning Center in Girard, Kan. She was a member of the First Christian Church in Webb City. Survivors include her husband, one daughter and two grandchildren. Her father, Charles Oster, also died in the tornado.

Cheryl E. Rantz, 62, of Carl Junction, was a lifetime area resident and worked as a tax preparer for H&R Block. She belonged to the Nazarene Church. She is survived by one daughter and two grandchildren.

Virgil "Tom" Reid, 77, of Columbus, Kan., was the retired owner of SEK Construction and a U.S. Army veteran. He was a member of the Hallowell World of Life Church. He enjoyed gardening, collecting coins, cooking, playing Dominos and finding recipes on the Internet. Survivors include his wife, five children, eight grandchildren and three great-grandchildren.

Johnnie Ray Richey, 52, of Joplin, worked for Allgeier, Martin & Associates for more than 30 years, most recently as a project engineer. He was a member of Joplin Elks Lodge No. 501 and did volunteer work at both Carl Richards bowling locations as well as Habitat for Humanity. He is survived by his son, Adam Richey, and his grandson, Griffin Richey.

Cayla Ann Selsor Robinson, 64, of Joplin, was a lifetime Southwest Missouri resident and a stay-at-home mom. She attended Frisco Church in Webb City and Forest Park Baptist Church in Joplin. She is survived by three daughters, one son, eight grandchildren and one great-grandchild, with another on the way.

Margaret Ellen Row, 50, of Joplin, had worked as a nurse at Mercy Hospital in Independence, Kan., at St. John's Regional Medical Center in Joplin and for hospice care. She collected clowns and piggy banks and enjoyed traveling. Survivors include her mother, three brothers and one sister.

Virginia Mae Salmon, 80, of Duquesne, was a fan of country and gospel music who loved spending time with her family. She also enjoyed shopping and telling stories of her childhood. Survivors include one daughter, four sons, 15 grandchildren, 28 great-grandchildren and five great-great-grandchildren.

Thomas Sarino, 75, of Joplin, lived alone. His family, including several children and grandchildren, lived in the Philippines.

Tonja Lee "Toni" Sawyer, 41, of Fort Scott, Kan., worked at Taco Bell in Fort Scott. She loved animals, painting, collecting antiques and writing short stories and poems. She attended the Apostolic Pentecostal Church. Survivors include her husband, Chad, whom she married five months ago, and her children.

Gladys J. Seay, 83, of Welch, Okla., was a licensed practical nurse and had worked at several hospitals in the Four-State Area. She was the family historian and spent hours in public libraries, studying family history. She was a member of the Church of Jesus Christ of Latter Day Saints in Miami. Survivors include two sons, two daughters, 13 grandchildren and 23 great-grandchildren.

Daniel Wayne Shirley, 48, of Joplin, traveled all over the United States and Canada as a salesman with a carnival. He moved to Goodman one year ago and had been living at the Greenbriar nursing home in Joplin since February. He enjoyed metal detector hunting, fishing and collecting knives and guns. He was a member of First Baptist Church in Pineville.

Judy Lee Smith, 71, of Joplin, owned and operated the Second Hand Rose Consignment Store. She was a member of St. Paul's United Methodist Church and loved reading, watching movies, shopping, and playing Trivial Pursuit and bridge. Survivors include two daughters, four grandchildren and three great-grandchildren.

Nicholaus Smith, 23, of Joplin, worked for Ozark Technical Ceramics. He moved to Joplin in February from his hometown of St. Louis. He and his brother, Chris, were interested in music and video production, and were preparing to open their own entertainment business as well as a hot-dog stand. He had also recently become engaged.

Shyrell Lee Smith, 68, of Pittsburg, Kan., was a registered nurse at Freeman Hospital East. She loved her work as a nurse and belonged to several organizations, including the Westside Church of the Nazarene, the Pittsburg Family YMCA and the American Red Cross. Survivors include a son, a daughter and four grandchildren.

Lois L. Sparks, 92, of Joplin, was married for 71 years to Wallace Sparks, who preceded her in death. She was a member of the Eastern Star, Harmony Heights Baptist Church and Eastview Baptist Church. Survivors include her son, Ralph Sparks, four grandchildren and eight great-grandchildren.

Steven J. Haack Stephens, 28, of Joplin, was a construction worker. He is survived by his wife, Tasha, and three children, Dayton Stephens, Alexander Haack Stephens and Alaris Haack Stephens.

Ralph Gilbert Stover, 85, of Miami, Okla., was a patient at St. John's Regional Medical Center when the tornado hit. He started Stover's Floor Covering in 1970 and retired from the business in 2001. He loved woodworking and gardening, and he belonged to the First United Methodist Church. Survivors include his wife, one son, two daughters, nine grandchildren and eight great-grandchildren.

Gregan D. Sweet, 59, of Joplin, had worked as a carpenter in residential building. He was a member of the Citywide Christian Fellowship and performed prison ministry. Survivors include his wife and two children

Jefferson Patrick Gerald Taylor, 31, of Kansas City, worked for the Riverside Department of Public Safety. He loved golf, coached his sons' soccer team and played softball with a team from work. He died of injuries sustained while assisting rescue efforts. Survivors include his wife, Kelly, and his sons, Caden and Cameron.

Kayleigh Savannah Teal, 16, of Seneca and Pittsburg, Kan., was a student at Seneca High School, where she loved her choir class. She was employed as a waitress at a Pizza Hut in Joplin. Survivors include her father, mother, three brothers and four sisters.

Heather Leigh Terry, 36, of Joplin, worked at LaBarge in Joplin. She had attended Aurora schools and was a lifetime resident of Southwest Missouri. She is survived by her husband, Michael.

John L. Thomas Jr., 40, of Joplin, was an employee of Jasper Products. He enjoyed playing golf, gambling, fishing, hunting, and playing football and catch. He was also known to love to work. He is survived by his four sons.

Zachary Delbert Treadwell, 9, of Joplin, was a third-grade student at Emerson Elementary School. He loved playing soccer, fishing and singing. He also was a fan of Pokemon, and his family said he was always telling elaborate stories and jokes. He is survived by his mother, father, brother and sister.

Margaret Ann Tutt, 92, of Joplin, was a volunteer with several local organizations, including the Blind Association, Meals on Wheels, Crosslines and Friends of the Library. She is survived by her daughter, two grandchildren and two great-grandchildren.

Michael Eugene Tyndall, 33, of Joplin, was a construction equipment operator and a 1997 graduate of Joplin High School. He was the father of three children, Kaylee Tyndall, Carson Tyndall and Arron Tyndall.

Darian "Dee" Vanderhoofven, 44, of Joplin, was the regional manager for the Heartland Lions Eye Bank. She loved to cook, work in her garden and entertain her friends. An animal lover, she often took in stray animals. She is survived by her husband, David; her son, Joshua, died with her in the storm.

Joshua Dean Vanderhoofven, 14 months, loved to watch "SpongeBob SquarePants" with his father, David. He also liked his bounce swing and his home, which he was just starting to explore after learning how to walk. He died with his mother, Dee, in the storm and is survived by his father, David.

Miguel Vasquez-Castillo, 29, of Joplin, was born in Mexico, where most of his family still lives. He was one of four children and described as the "life of the party" by Monica Lopez, who worked with him at the El Vaquero restaurant in Joplin. His girlfriend, Maria Alvarez-Torres, also died in the tornado.

M. "Dean" Wells, 59, of Webb City, was a department head at the Home Depot store on Range Line Road, where he ushered several of his customers and co-workers to safety when the tornado hit. He was retired from the U.S. Army and was the married father of two adult daughters and grandfather of four children. He loved to whistle and had made at least two CDs of his whistling.

Tiera Nicole Whitley, 20, of Fort Scott, Kan., was a 2009 graduate of Jayhawk Linn High School who was employed as a shift manager at Taco Bell in Fort Scott. She was a talented artist and photographer who enjoyed fishing and woodworking. Survivors include her parents, one sister and one brother.

Regina Mae Bloxham Williams, 55, of Joplin, was a customer service representative for AT&T. She moved to Joplin in 2002 from Carthage and was a member of the AT&T Pioneers. Survivors include her husband, three daughters, two sons and two grandchildren.

Zachary Allen Williams, 12, of Joplin, was a seventh-grader at East Middle School who attended Calvary Baptist Church. He enjoyed Hot Wheels cars, Legos, riding his bike and spending time with his friends. He had been looking forward to his summer vacation, when he planned to spend time with his family and read some of his favorite books. He is survived by his mother, father and brother.

Charles William Writer, 74, of Purdy, retired from the U.S. Navy in 1964 after 10 years of service. He later worked for Pryor Motor Co. and owned the DX Gas Station, High Point Trucking Co. and a transport truck leasing company. He also farmed cattle and enjoyed working with his horses. He is survived by his wife, four sons, four daughters, 18 grandchildren and 22 great-grandchildren.

Barbara Ann Anderson, 76, of Joplin, was a resident of the Greenbriar nursing home and a former licensed practical nurse. She also enjoyed fishing. She is survived by a son, a daughter, four grandchildren and six great-grandchildren.

Dale Arsenault, 52, of Springfield, was a resident of the Greenbriar nursing home. He was a drywall technician who grew up in Long Beach, Calif., and moved to Springfield about 17 years ago. He had worked on several Springfield-based construction projects including the Bass Pro store and the Hammons Field stadium. Survivors include his mother.

Dorthey C. Bell, 88, of Joplin, had taught school and enjoyed traveling, bird-watching, reading and genealogy. She was active in the Joplin Family Y and was a member of the Order of the Eastern Star and Central City Christian Church. Survivors include three sons and five grandchildren.

Barbara Boyd, 87, of Joplin, was a resident of the Greenbriar nursing home. She worked for more than 20 years in the burn unit of a Veterans Administration hospital in Richmond, Va. She liked to crochet and belonged to the First Baptist Church in Joplin. She is survived by two sons, two daughters and six grandchildren.

Burnice M. Bresee, 91, of Joplin, was a homemaker and member of Christ Point Church. Survivors include two sons, four daughters, 18 grandchildren, 34 great-grandchildren and four great-great-grandchildren.

Edmon A. Cooper, 88, of Joplin, was a U.S. Army veteran of World War II. He previously worked as a mechanic with farm equipment for Massey Ferguson and retired in 1995 from Vollenweider Orchid in Exeter. Survivors include two children, 11 grandchildren, 13 great-grandchildren and one great-great-grandchild.

Vicki L. Cooper, 58, of Joplin.

Alice L. Hudson Cope, 79, of Neosho, was a seamstress and an avid reader. She held a degree in archaeology and had participated in a dig in Israel. She also loved studying the Bible and was a member of First Christian Church in Neosho. Survivors include her son, her daughter, three grandchildren and two great-grandchildren.

Michael Wayne Dennis, 52, of Galena, Kan., was a patient at St. John's Regional Medical Center when the tornado hit. He was disabled and never worked, and he enjoyed comic books and PlayStation. Survivors include his uncles and cousins.

Mark L. Farmer, 56, of Joplin, had worked at Joplin Workshops for more than 20 years. His friends and roommates, Rick Fox and Tripp Miller, died with him in the storm.

Ida M. Finley, 88, of Joplin, was a warehouse worker for years in Ohio before moving to Joplin in 2009. She was a widow and the mother of one son, with three grandchildren, one great-grandchild and two great-great-grandchildren.

Rick E. Fox, 56, of Joplin, was an employee of Joplin Workshops since 1976 and an accomplished bowler who was a member of the Special Olympics bowling team. He also was a member of Calvary Baptist Church and attended First Presbyterian Church. He is survived by his mother, Doris Fox.

Marsha Ann Frost, 32, of Joplin, was a member of the Christian Life Center in Joplin who had been employed by Wal-Mart in Bentonville, Ark. Survivors include a son, Gabriel Frost. Her son Sebastian died with her in the storm.

Sebastian Charles Frost, 10, of Joplin, was a member of the Christian Life Center. He is survived by his father, Roger Frost, and his brother, Gabriel. His mother, Marsha, died with him in the storm.

Judy R. Head.

Kenneth James Henson, 56, of Miami, Okla., was a master machinist. He is survived by one son, James Henson, and one grandchild, Jadyn Dihel.

Ronnie D. Holloway, 68, of Joplin.

Charlotte Hopwood, 84, of Joplin.

Iona Lee Hull, 70, of Carthage, was a homemaker. Survivors include two daughters, nine grandchildren and 13 great-grandchildren.

Dorothy M. Johnston, 91, of Joplin, retired as vice president of Tanner Brothers Inc., a road construction company, where she served as the first female board member. Survivors include her sister and several nieces and nephews.

Tedra Jewell Kuhn, 69, of Joplin, was a homemaker who loved her family. She also enjoyed going to the casino, and she always had a smile on her face and cared for others before herself. Survivors include two children, two grandchildren and several great-grandchildren.

Billie Sue Huff Little, 65, of Joplin, a waitress, is survived by her daughter, Tammy Curtner, and a grandson, Donnie Reed.

Rachel K. Markham, 31, of Joplin.

Nancy Ann Martin, 52, of Neosho, was a lifelong Neosho resident and graduate of Neosho High School. She worked as a caregiver at the New Vision Group Home. She is survived by her sons, Anthony Owen and Brandon Martin, and one granddaughter, Khristeena Owen.

Janice Kay McKee, 60, of Wyandotte, Okla., was a resident of the Greenbriar nursing home. She is survived by her husband, Gary; her son, Gary Jr.; and one granddaughter, ShaKetha.

Mary Lois Lovell McKeel, 65, of Joplin, was a retired cafeteria cook for the Carl Junction School District. Her husband, James, died with her in the storm. Survivors include two sons, a daughter, three grandchildren and one great-grandchild.

Ronald D. Meyer, 64, of Joplin, was a former night auditor for hotels before becoming a full-time care provider for his brother, George. He was a U.S. Air Force veteran who served in the Vietnam War. Survivors include three brothers and one sister.

Lorna "Kay" Miller, 72, of Joplin, had lived most of her life in Kansas and was retired from the food service industry, where she had worked as a waitress, grocery store clerk and school cafeteria cook. She enjoyed sewing, reading and bird-watching, and she loved nature and cats. Survivors include one daughter and two grandchildren.

Suzanne M. Mock, 39, of Forsyth, is survived by her husband, Thomas Mock, her son, Thomas J. Mock, and her daughters, Amber Mock and Amanda Mock. She also had two grandchildren.

Doris Marie Menhusen Montgomery, 83, of Joplin, was a former teacher in Kansas and returned to Joplin two years ago to be near her children. She attended Christ's Community United Methodist Church. She is survived by three daughters, a son, nine grandchildren, 12 great-grandchildren and nine great-great-grandchildren.

Estrellita M. Moore, 64, of Joplin, was a hairdresser at J.C. Penney. She attended St. Mary's Catholic Church and loved going to the casino.

Sally Ann Moulton, 58, of Joplin, was a U.S. Air Force veteran of the Vietnam War and had worked for the Veterans Service Office and the Health and Housing Department, both of Belleville, Ill. She was interested in theater and was performing in the Stained Glass Theatre when the tornado hit. She also loved trivia and writing poetry. Survivors include a daughter.

Mary Joyce Perry, 76, of Joplin, was a lifetime Joplin resident. She worked for C.J.'s Uniforms in Joplin and was a former secretary for Prudential Insurance and KODE-TV. She enjoyed spending time with her family. Survivors include one daughter, one son, two grandsons and two great-grandchildren.

Anna Pettek, 91, of Joplin, was a resident of the Greenbriar nursing home.

Troy Raney, 39, of Joplin.

Darlene Kay (Hall) Ray, 63, of Galena, Kan., was a patient at St. John's Regional Medical Center when the tornado hit. She was a former King Louie Manufacturing employee who enjoyed playing bingo at Bordertown Casino. Survivors include her husband, Wesley, and her son, Steven.

Vicki Patrice Robertson, 66, of Joplin, is survived by her children, Mike Johnson, Danny Robertson, Joe Robertson, Dannielle Robertson and Ardis Robertson.

Keith Derek Robinson, 50, of Joplin, was a certified nursing assistant at the Greenbriar nursing home and a former employee of Freeman Hospital West. He had a stern but kind manner of motivating his patients during their rehabilitation and enjoyed watching old movies. Survivors include his mother, one sister and one brother.

Grace Marie Sanders, 82, of Carthage, was a patient at St. John's Regional Medical Center when the tornado hit. She had worked as a bookkeeper for many years at the Joplin Stockyards. She is survived by her husband of nearly 65 years, Robert.

Frances Ann Scates, 71, of Joplin, was a member of St. John's Lutheran Church in Freistatt. She is survived by two sons, three daughters, 11 grandchildren and six great-grandchildren.

Gene Smith, 71, of Joplin, was a U.S. Navy veteran who loved Webb City football and the St. Louis Cardinals. He worked for the Union Pacific Railroad for 24 years and was a member of the Webb City Church of the Nazarene, the Joplin Eagles Lodge and the Greater Joplin U.S. Bowling Congress. He is survived by his wife, one son, one daughter and two grandsons.

Betty J. Stogsdill, 83, of Joplin, taught high school for many years in Chicago and was later a substitute teacher for the Joplin School District. She loved the theater and belonged to Forest Park Baptist Church. Survivors include her sister and several nieces and nephews.

J.T. Strickland, 86, of Joplin, was a retired U.S. Navy veteran who had served during World War II and the Korean War. He had also worked as a motel manager and attended Peace Lutheran Church. Survivors include his wire, one daughter, five grandchildren and 10 great-grandchildren

Sandra Thomas, 55, of Carthage, was an employee of Justin Boots for 20 years. She graduated from Carthage High School in 1974 and was a member of the Joplin Full Gospel Church, where she volunteered in the nursery. She is survived by her parents and her sister; a niece, Natalia Puebla, also died in the storm.

Douglas Williams, 52, of Purdy, moved to Southwest Missouri in 2005. He enjoyed raising horses and spending time in his garden with his dog, Tuff. Survivors include his wife, Leah, daughter, Randi, and four step-daughters.

Chapter Eleven

WINDS OF CHANGE

ONE HUNDRED DAYS AFTER THE tornado, the debris which had littered the landscape from one end of town to the other had been cleared away, leaving an empty, treeless swath that would provide the foundation for the area's rebirth.

Volunteers and donations continued to pour into the city, aiding in recovery efforts.

In what seemed a daunting challenge when plans were announced, Joplin students returned to school on schedule; with the district stating their goal of having schools rebuilt within three years. St. John's announced a $950 million project to build a new hospital. About 370 of 500 businesses that were in the tornado's path had reopened, the Joplin Area Chamber of Commerce reported. Another 50, including Home Depot and the Wal-Mart Supercenter on 15th Street, were under construction.

Hundreds of permits for residential and business construction were filed in just the month of June, as work got under way to rebuild.

The winds – which, in just 32 minutes, forever changed the landscape of Joplin on the evening of May 22 – have yet to stop blowing.

"I will never forget what I saw. In addition to the loss of 162 lives and 8,000 homes, the Federal Emergency Management Agency lead in Joplin told me that there is more wreckage in the town than there was at Ground Zero after Sept. 11, 2001. As stunning as that magnitude might be, the response has been equally stunning."

— *AmeriCorps Director John Gomperts.*

"It feels like we're finally moving past the sad part of all of this and getting to something that is happy. The tornado, it seems, stole several months away from us of our lives and our happiness, and we've come to a place where we're ready to put it to rest and move on.

— *Monica Mihajlovic, whose family took shelter in the laundry room of their home on S. Connor Avenue as the tornado tore their home apart around them.*

"At 23 and learning how to walk again, that's kind of a big deal. I stand up as much as possible because it's nice to be that height again. I have accepted it; there's nothing else you can do."

— *Matt Stephens, whose left leg was amputated due to injuries sustained in the tornado.*

OPPOSITE: Ron Hankins, an equipment operator with C.K. Construction of Diamond, tears down the remains of a home damaged in the tornado in the 2000 block of Annie Baxter Avenue. *Photo by T. Rob Brown*

LEFT: Flags, such as this one blowing in front of St. Mary's church, became a prominent symbol of patriotism and unity in the days after the May 22 tornado. *Photo by B.W. Shepherd*

"I guess you go back to the old (Charles) Dickens quote: 'It was the best of times; it was the worst of times.' In spite of the fact that you were dealing with a terrible tragedy, the 'love thy neighbor' philosophy was very much intact here in Joplin."

— *C.J. Huff, superintendent of the Joplin School District.*

"Joplin is the toughest town on God's green Earth. Those who have answered the call here are heroes."

— *Gov. Jay Nixon.*

"We see things moving forward every day. To me, it's unbelievable it has moved so fast. I just didn't see how that would happen."

— *Ken Martin, president of the Great Plains Federal Credit Union, one of the businesses on Range Line damaged in the tornado.*

"We haven't seen it this busy in six or seven years at least. I foresee this for three, five, seven years. There are lot of homes to rebuild. This is not something that is going to happen overnight."

— *Mike Landis, a Joplin homebuilder.*

"I've seen no better response. The recovery effort has been swift and thorough. The city has done an incredible job of envisioning what is needed for the future and for handling the day-to-day operations. That does not always happen in disasters."

— *Libby Turner, FEMA's federal coordinating officer for the disaster.*

"This will be a national event. We will have 8,000 to 10,000 volunteers working all day and all night for a week. But the build will be about the families, the heroes. It will be much more than just home building."

— *Sam Clifton, president of Millstone Custom Homes, of Springfield, announcing that "Extreme Makeover: Home Edition" was planning a "big build" in Joplin.*

LEFT: Max Bass, of Vinita, Okla., helps clean up a dry pond bed at Parr Hill Park. Bass was a member of a volunteer group with the Church of Jesus Christ of Latter Day Saints that came to Joplin to volunteer. *Photo by T. Rob Brown*

OPPOSITE TOP: Meagen Duffee, an assistant naturalist with Nature Reach at Pittsburg State University, releases a red-tailed hawk back into the wild. Phoenix, as it was named, was found after the tornado and rescued from beneath the rubble. *Photo by T. Rob Brown*

OPPOSITE BOTTOM: Sixteen-year-old Steven Weersing shows off the tattoo of his last name on his forearm that helped his father, David, identify him after the tornado. Steven, who suffered critical injuries, was released from Children's Mercy Hospital in Kansas City on Sept. 2. *Photo by Kellen Jenkins*

BELOW: (From left) Stephanie Meek, Susan Myers and Kathleen Mertens walk through tornado-stricken neighborhoods to visit with residence and offer assistance. The three women are community crisis workers with Ozark Crisis Center. *Photo by T. Rob Brown*

"You're going to have one interesting story to tell your baby."

— *Desiree Rogers, recalling what a firefighter told her as she was freed from underneath broken slabs of concrete at Dillons on May 22. Her baby, due in January, was unharmed.*

"I think the biggest accomplishment we've achieved is our coming together as a community."

— *Mayor Mike Woolston.*

"We are making this commitment because it's the right thing to do for Joplin."

— *Lynn Britton, president and chief executive officer of Mercy Health, announcing the new location for St. John's Mercy, near Interstate 44 and Main Street. The new hospital is scheduled to open in 2014.*

"I've always been told that you can't predict what will happen, but this really helped drive that point home.

Things are replaceable, but life is a little more delicate than that."

— *Corey Hounschell, who was among the 445 graduates of Joplin High School on the afternoon of May 22.*

"The city of Joplin has benefited from the presence of approximately 85,000 registered volunteers in helping us recover from the tragic effects of the May 22, 2011 tornado. It's estimated that twice as many have aided the city by going directly into the storm-damaged area to render assistance. That means a quarter million people have braved oppressive heat and less than ideal conditions overall to assist us in our recovery ...This is the fundamental example of the 'Miracle of the Human Spirit' that I often refer to. It has reaffirmed my faith in mankind. I know there is a volunteer state, but I think the occurrences of the last three months insures Joplin's place as the volunteer city."

— *Mark Rohr, city manager.*

ABOVE: Keith Stammer (left), Jasper County's emergency management director, and Kelly Stammer, of Parsons, walk through a row of temporary homes brought in by FEMA. The site was named the Officer Jeff Taylor Memorial Acres. *Photo by Roger Nomer*

RIGHT: Tanner Hodges (right), of Joplin, helps whip up a parachute as other students run across it. Held on Aug. 10 at Missouri Southern, the "I Am Joplin" event was designed to bring together school-age children and their families to celebrate before classes began for the year. *Photo by T. Rob Brown*

ABOVE: James Shipley, owner of Shipley Masonry, works on restoring the chimney of a home on South Brownell Avenue. *Photo by B.W. Shepherd*

RIGHT: Gov. Jay Nixon and his wife, Georganne, get a tour of the temporary high school at Northpark Mall from Superintendent C.J. Huff. The 2011-12 school year opened on schedule, just 87 days after the tornado. *Photo by T. Rob Brown*

ABOVE: Actor and comedian David Koechner was among those who performed during the "Stand Up for Joplin" show held on July 19 in Taylor Performing Arts Center. He was joined by Brett Butler, Yakov Smirnoff and others. *Photo by Roger Nomer*

ABOVE: Conrad Proctor, 7, a Joplin second-grader, watches as educators enter Taylor Performing Arts Center during an Aug. 15 kickoff for the new school year. *Photo by T. Rob Brown*

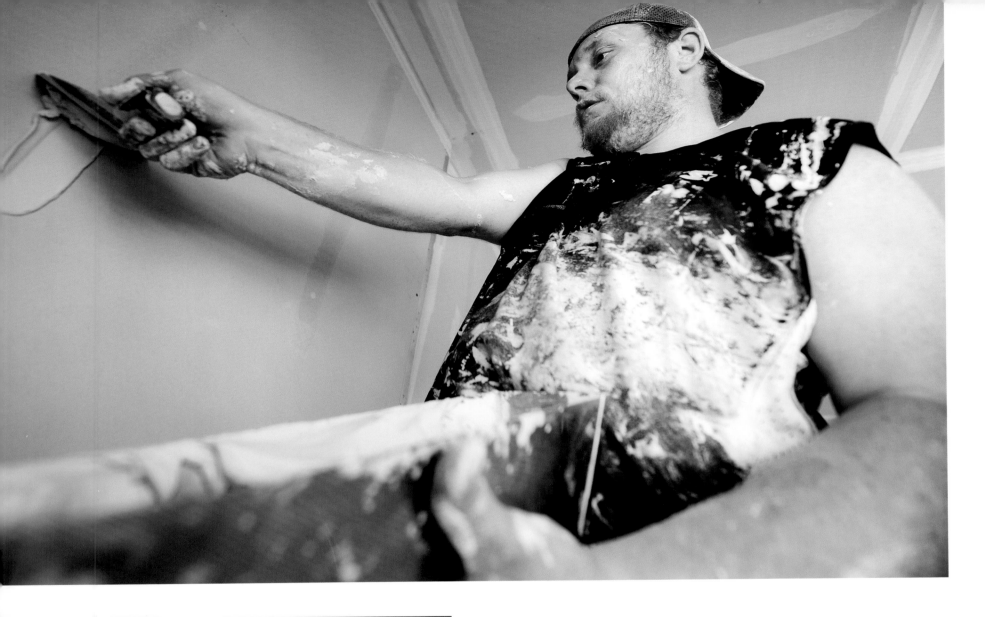

ABOVE: Cody Berry, a drywall finisher with OT's Quality Drywall Inc., works inside the garage of a home being rebuilt on Byers Avenue. *Photo by T. Rob Brown*

LEFT: Adam Deberry, owner of Affordable Tile & Roofing of Webb City, carries a board across a new roof being built on a home near the intersection of 23rd Street and Pearl Avenue. *Photo by T. Rob Brown*

ABOVE: Levi Koch, 14, a Boy Scout from Troop 55 in Lawrence, Kan., helps sort through debris on the Joplin High School football field. On Aug. 6, more than 900 Boy Scouts from across the country came to Joplin to help with relief efforts. *Photo by Roger Nomer*

RIGHT: Elks Lodge member Randy Bell rakes up debris on lodge property before mowing the grass. With trees and homes taken by the storm, the remnants of St. John's can be seen behind him. *Photo by B.W. Shepherd*

ABOVE: Becky Ashcraft cradles her cat, Ducky, after being reunited on Aug. 2. Ducky was found living at the site of the former Hampshire Terrace apartments by a volunteer animal rescue group.

Photo by B.W. Shepherd

LEFT: Tiffany Falley, an early childhood educator with Martin Luther School, looks through educational materials during a school supply event at The Bridge. Teachers from across the nation donated classroom supplies to help local educators get ready for school.

Photo by Roger Nomer

131

ABOVE: Evening settles on the rows of FEMA mobile homes that were set up across from the Joplin Regional Airport. *Photo by B.W. Shepherd*

ABOVE: Iriving Elementary second-grader Maguire Mai shows some enthusiasm during the first day of school. *Photo by Roger Nomer*

LEFT: While attending a therapeutic art class at the Wildcat Glades Conservation & Audbuon Center, Tatum Goetteo drew a picture of her dream back yard – complete with a tornado shelter. *Photo by B.W. Shepherd*

RIGHT: Joyce Richey was reunited with her son's dog, Sugar, 12 weeks after the tornado. Her son, John Richey, was among the 162 fatalities. She said she hoped finding Sugar could help bring some closure.

Photo by B.W. Shepherd

ABOVE: Seen from the intersection of Prairie Flower Road and Highway 171, lights from FEMA mobile homes shine brightly against the night sky. *Photo by B.W. Shepherd*

ABOVE: A quarter moon rises over the remains of a home on the 2300 block of Virginia Avenue, three months after the tornado struck Joplin. *Photo by B.W. Shepherd*

The Power to Rebuild Joplin

At **Empire District Electric Company,**
we are dedicated to providing
the power to rebuild Joplin.

www.empiredistrict.com

EMPIRE

SERVICES YOU COUNT ON

OUR COMMUNITY...
OUR CAMPUS...
OUR PRIDE!

Proud to be a part of
the Joplin Community...

Now & Always!

MSSU
MISSOURI SOUTHERN STATE UNIVERSITY

www.mssu.edu • 1.866.818.MSSU (6778)

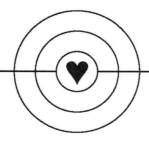

The Heart to recover. The Energy to rebuild.

Joplin's extraordinary renaissance is powered

by the most inexhaustible fuel on earth:

THE HUMAN SPIRIT.

The employees of MGE salute you for your

compassion, your resilience, and your

collective will to recover after the storm.

As long as that incredible community spirit

stays lit, the future will always be bright.

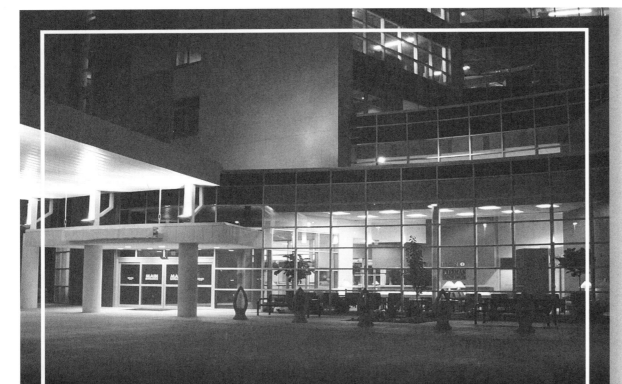